JESUS, LORD AND CHRIST

JESUS, LORD AND CHRIST

by

John F. O'Grady

PAULIST PRESS
New York / Paramus / Toronto

NIHIL OBSTAT:
Joseph J. Grabys, S.T.D.
Censor Librorum

IMPRIMATUR:
✝ Edwin B. Broderick, D.D., Ph.D.
Bishop of Albany

October 2, 1972

The Nihil Obstat and Imprimatur are official declarations that a book
or pamphlet is free of doctrinal or moral error. No implication is con-
tained therein that those who have granted the Nihil Obstat and
Imprimatur agree with the contents, opinions or statements expressed.

Library of Congress
Catalog Card Number: 72-94395

ISBN 0-8091-1765-7

Cover design by Morris Berman
Cover drawing by Rita Corbin

Published by Paulist Press
Editorial Office: 1865 Broadway, N.Y., N.Y. 10023
Business Office: 400 Sette Drive, Paramus, N.J. 07652

Printed and bound in the
United States of America

CONTENTS

To
Joseph P. McClain
and my many friends in the
Diocese of Albany

PREFACE

"Who do you say that I am?" and Peter answered: "You are the Christ" (Mk 8:29-30). This question was important for the disciples of Jesus Christ. It is a question which was addressed not only to them, but which is addressed to each believer today. We have to make a response to that question, and it is a difficult response. We can say as easily as Peter said, "You are the Christ," or "You are the Son of God," or "You are the Savior," or "You are the Lord." But what does it mean?

The only way anyone can respond to a question such as "Who do you say that I am?" is to enter into a deep relationship with this person, Jesus Christ. You never know someone unless you have made the effort to try to understand the person. So it is much more complicated than just saying "You are the Christ." If there is a purpose for this book, it is to pose the question from the gospel of Mark, "Who do you say that I am?" If we go further from there and talk about the goal as far as these chapters are concerned, the goal is always going to be a response, but it is going to have to be a personal response. Individuals are the ones who are going to have to say something to that question and no one can say it for someone else.

We can turn to the scriptures and try to see how other people have responded to this question because that is what the New Testament is, a personal testimony of faith in Jesus of Nazareth, made through a community. This will help us a great deal. But in another sense it is going to leave us a little confused, as there were many groups of people responding to this question so we are going to end up with many christologies in the New Testament. There are as many responses to that question "Who

1

do you say that I am?" as there are people and Christian com-
munities who hear the question. So the goal is very specific;
it is to help a believer make a personal response to this question.
Why bother to do this? This is another question we can ask.
Not too many people are concerned with the question of Christ
today. If anything, they are concerned with the question of God.
Does he exist? What is he like? How can we know God? But
more accurately, people are not even interested in the question
of God. The great concern today that is being offered to each
one by the world in which we live is not the question of God,
nor the question of Christ, but it is the question of man, or the
question of human life. What is the relationship that exists
between people? What is the meaning of life? How can a person become other than what he is and what role can God play
in the development of a human life? A change seems to have
taken over society. There is often a gloom that persists with
more and more people wondering and questioning and failing
to come to a response. Change frightens people. Events happen too fast. How can one remain warm and human in the
midst of a society that is becoming less than human? Is there a
future to give to children or are we all helping to destroy ourselves? The responses of past ages do not seem to ring true
and so puzzlement and confusion characterize our age.

   If the whole question today is the meaning of man and the
purpose of life and not the meaning of God, then why bother
to talk about Jesus Christ? We talk about Jesus, the Christ, because to discover him is to discover man. The more we understand this fascinating individual of long ago, the more we understand ourselves. He offers an approach to life that can bring
meaning and purpose and take away the gloom.

   In spite of what is written above, there is interest in Jesus
today, but not in the Son of God as the Word incarnate with
the emphasis on the divinity of Jesus, but an interest in the
man—Jesus of Nazareth. This fits well the spirit that seems to
pervade society today.

   If people question life and its meaning, it is helpful to believe
that once there was a man who gave a distinct response to

the meaning of life and this man was Jesus Christ. If we can possibly come to a better understanding of him and how he lived his life, we have the possibility of understanding ourselves differently and we may come to a realization of the value of living, as he did.

The purpose of these chapters is to pose a question, a personal question which has to be directed individually and the response must be a personal response which means that there will be as many responses as there are people who make that response. It will be the reader's response and no one else can make it.

It can be asked, for whom is this work intended? The response to this question will be very simple. If people are crying for someone to offer a meaning in life and if Jesus Christ can do this, then his ministers, his teachers and followers must know and understand more about him and develop the ability to communicate their appreciation of him to others. This book is intended for all those who have belief in Jesus Christ and want to grow in that belief; it is particularly directed to those who are engaged in leading others to that belief.

The orientation will be biblical since it is all there, but the emphasis will be on the lived experience of believers who are called to make this biblical Christ live today.

Finally, it can be said words, ideas and books are not the creation of one person. This book, the words used and ideas expressed are not the exclusive property of the author. Much of what is written has been learned from teachers, from books, from students and from friends. It is returned to them in written form.

No effort to present a full dogmatic treatment of Christology is intended in these pages. It is offered as theological reflections based on the gospels and directed to the needs of believers today. It is hoped that what is written will find a receptive audience in those who would like to understand more about belief in Jesus, the Christ.

The chief encouragement for this book has been given by Mrs. Eleanor Bolduc who chided the author into working and acted as a supporting critic and typist. To her and to the students of the Seminary of Our Lady of Angels who first heard these thoughts, I am profoundly indebted and offer sincerest gratitude.

Albany, New York, 1972

CHAPTER 1
BIBLICAL CHRISTOLOGY

To try to explain precisely what biblical Christology means is not an easy task. If we admit that we are not sure exactly what biblical theology means, then there is also uncertainty about what biblical Christology means. It would be an easier task if the Bible were only a divinely written book, but this is not true. Just as we speak of the Word of God become man as divine and human, so we have to say much the same in regard to Sacred Scripture with all the conclusions and consequences of the union of two elements which cannot be separated or confused. In spite of the difficulties it can be said that biblical Christology seeks to gather and propose in a certain systematic fashion all those things which Sacred Scripture says of Jesus of Nazareth in his person and his work in an effort to understand both better.

Since we cannot consider all the various aspects of Christ in the gospels there will have to be a selection but the selection will be based on today's needs: we desire to make it possible for the Spirit to be heard today. What does the Spirit say to the churches of Christ? And so we select, based on the demands of the present time and based on the progress in the understanding of faith today. A review of biblical methodology will help.[1]

The Bible is the *gospel of the living God* since by divine and human authority it was written at a certain time so that it would remain and in its own way be the measure and norm (written norm) of faith and thus of the understanding of this faith. The gospel is not primarily doctrine, but life, a conscious

5

life, a truly human life, to be lived and understood, freely and actively, according to the understanding given by God so that if this is accepted, life is fulfilled and effective and fruitful.

The Bible is also the first *human testimony of the gospel* given by God orally. It is the personal testimony of a gospel that was accepted personally and esteemed and loved. At the same time it is the human testimony of the Word of God today, announcing, explaining, affirming God himself and his self-gift to man so that we today ought always to listen to and hear and accept with esteem and love what we have received.

The Bible as the Word of God is a *human document;* it was written over a period of years by certain individual men. It is the documentation of those writers who wished to pass on as from God a gospel, each in his own way. The Bible then is the documentation of certain writers themselves (or at least of their contemporaries) of those things which they perceived with their senses, their intellect and heart. It is the record of all of those things which they experienced as men, with all the sensibilities which make up a human experience. After their experience they thought about it, searched over the experience and with their own genius committed to writing what had been theirs with a determined reason and with a determined scope. We must recall that in the perception and in the documentation there was something *personal* which is true of anything in human life. But this does not falsify what was presented since this is how we all live and this is how God desired to share his Word with us.

We also must recall that there was *inspiration* regarding Sacred Scripture. God desires to speak through human words, but precisely these words and not others. The writings of Ignatius of Antioch or the Didache are from the same period but are not Sacred Scripture. God did not want to give us completely an objective book since this is impossible but he did want to speak to us through some books in a different way than others.

And so we can say that the Sacred Scriptures are full of humanity and as such are tainted with humanity which means a sinful humanity. This is no surprise for if God chose to come to a sinful man he also chose sinful man in the expression of his Word in the Sacred Scriptures.

All of these notions must be applied to biblical Christology. It is not sufficient to say that the New Testament is the documentation of the members of the Christian community made by them after they had the experience of the risen Lord inasmuch as they believed in him. This is true but not sufficient. Sacred Scripture is also inspired which makes it living for us. We cannot just seek the genius or the intention of the human authors and what they wished to give us but must also ask what God wishes to tell us through this book. Only in the midst of a living faith can we come to any notion of biblical Christology. To be more specific, we must speak of the relationship between Jesus and human history, the gospel as heard and announced and the lack of a complete biblical Christology.

Jesus and Human History

The Bible stands in a line of the divine actions in human history. We have to use categories of history and philosophy to interpret his actions as in all that God does. The reason is that Jesus Christ is divine but truly man and so he is historical, living within an historical people, and indeed in the line of expectation and preparation which sought salvation. Jesus showed himself as historical, as the fulfillment of promises, but at the same time as one who was to come again. He is the end and culmination of human history but history must continue after his time on earth and so he stands as part of human history and at the same time transcends it.

Thus it must be admitted that it is extremely difficult to find any method of presentation which is fitting for the presentation of those things which Sacred Scripture says of the person and work of Jesus. The documents that we have are the record of a certain experience of Jesus, Son of God and man, by his disciples. The Bible then participates in the mystery of God himself and that means that we may end up knowing less than we think. Even after 2000 years, with the assistance of the

Spirit, we can offer no adequate theological vision of the mystery of Christ and so we cannot expect a complete Christology in the primitive documents. Even in Sacred Scripture we cannot expect to find a complete harmony of doctrines or sayings of Jesus since they come from a specific time and they are human, with all the defects of anything human. Thus in interpretation we have to pay close attention to the historical ambit, the social, cultural and religious milieu of men of that time and in that place.

The Gospel as Heard and Announced

Since God chose to act with man in a human way it should not be considered a marvel if the gospel was circumscribed and announced by certain spiritual ideas common to all men. The Word was made man, a Jew, who was born on a certain day and lived in a specific country, Israel. What he did and what he taught are seen as human, taken from that time, in that region. The same is true for all the men to whom he spoke and with whom he lived. They are real people of a particular education and culture and time. If Jesus spoke of God he did so as he understood him and his listeners responded with an understanding of God as they knew him. If he spoke of Father, they thought of father as they knew fathers. And so the announcement of the gospel was clearly limited by the people and events which surrounded Jesus of Nazareth.

Something similar could be said about the preaching of the gospel. The first listeners were Jews and Greeks. What they heard they heard as men and women of their own culture. Each tried to understand in a certain harmony and unity what he had experienced and compared this new "thing" or way with what he had previously experienced. The new experience of faith in Jesus Christ was integrated into the human personality with the formulation in their own way and with their own categories. All of this brings us to an appreciation of the diversity in understanding and expressions of the one gospel.[2]

What makes matters more difficult for us is that even after

2000 years we do not have a full biblical Christology. We have
a lot of ideas and isolated studies but no complete Christology
based on the Bible and having said all of this we return to
the decision to try to offer a biblical Christology that makes
sense today.[3]

No one can doubt that Christ is the heart of Christianity but
there is a purpose behind the coming of Christ seen in the
Bible that is more fundamental. He is the final manifestation
of God and leads men to God as Father. Paul reminds us that
he is the "first born of all brethren" but also that in the end he
will hand his kingdom over to the Father and He will be all
in all. If we come to appreciate Christ and have faith in him,
it is ultimately to lead us to the Father and in that sense, biblical Christology is to make us more conscious of our relationship
to God as Father. To go further, as already mentioned, this is a
personal study of Jesus which demands a questioning attitude
on the part of each believer. If we knew all the answers there
would be no need for further study. The question upon which
these pages are based is the same question which Jesus addressed to his disciples: "Who do you say that I am?" The
response that Jesus wanted of his disciples is the same response
he wants today: a response of living and sincere faith: "You
are the Son of the living God." Jesus of Nazareth is the Son
of the God of Abraham, Isaac and Jacob, the God of Socrates
and Aristotle, the God of Gandhi, Martin Luther King, Pope
John and John Kennedy, the God of yesterday, and today and
tomorrow. This is the response expected of us as we treat him
who for us and for our salvation lived with us as the Word of
God incarnate, and whose glory we have seen. We begin our
brief study of the mystery of Jesus hearing and seeking to
understand, being willing to be evangelized as we listen to the
prayer of St. Paul to the Father:

That is why I kneel before the Father from whom every family
in heaven and on earth takes its name; and I pray that he will
bestow on you gifts in keeping with the riches of his glory. May
he strengthen you inwardly through the working of his Spirit.
May Christ dwell in your hearts through faith, and may charity
be the root and foundation of your life. Thus you will be able

to grasp fully, with all the holy ones, the breadth and length and height and depth of Christ's love, and experience this love which surpasses all knowledge, so that you may attain to the fullness of God himself.

To him whose power now at work in us can do immeasurably more than we ask or imagine—to him be glory in the church and in Christ Jesus through all generations,. world without end. Amen. (Eph 3:14-20)

Jesus in the Bible

If Jesus of Nazareth is to make sense today then we have to see him as he is found in the gospels. If we are to make the response in faith to the question: "Who do you say that I am?" then we have to see him as he comes to us today. What is there in Jesus Christ that speaks to us today? We will try to respond to this question by a brief analysis of his attitudes toward life and events and aspects of life.

Jesus, the Devout Jew [4]

Jesus as a devout Jew offers a possibility to remain faithful to the traditions of centuries in the midst of great change. He was born into the Jewish religion with all its glories as well as its narrowness. He showed a deep respect for this religion and abided by many of its prescriptions. His preaching was limited almost exclusively to the borders of Palestine; he went to the temple on the major feasts; understood and respected the Torah and used it for his response in morality. He accepted the baptism of John for repentance and waited and worked for the coming of the Kingdom of God. He had a zeal for the House of the Lord and asked that the dictates of the law be fulfilled. He admonished his followers to give Caesar what was surely Caesar's: "Love your enemies;" "Do not resist evil;" "Turn the other cheek;" in all he offered the best of what was tradition in a life that can only be seen as the life of a devout

Jew of the first century. However, he was also a free man in his devotion.

Jesus, the Free Man [5]

Jesus knew and loved his traditions, but he interpreted them freely. He respected the Sabbath but always within bounds. He cured on the Sabbath (Lk 6:7); he allowed his disciples to pick grain on the Sabbath (Lk 6:1). He fulfilled the demands of the law when the law helped people, but would not worry about eating with unclean hands, especially when people fulfilled this prescription but left their hearts unclean (Mt 7:1-23). He accepted social customs and told the leper to go and fulfill what is demanded by Moses and show himself to the high priest (Lk 5:14); but Jesus broke social custom when it was inhuman. He gladly spoke to sinners and publicans because they needed him (Lk 5:31). For Jesus, the law was the expression of the love of God and neighbor:

"You shall love the Lord your God with all your heart and with all your soul and with all your mind. This is the great and first commandment. And a second is like it. You shall love your neighbor as yourself. On these two commandments depend all the law and the prophets." (Mt 22:38-40)

This was the basic law with every situation and interpretation founded on the fundamental love of God and neighbor. Jesus was free in regard to law because he interpreted the law in the light of love of neighbor.

Such freedom challenged the Jewish system. Yet Jesus tells his followers he has come not to destroy the law but to fulfill the law (Mt 5:17). What he offers is not a new law but a new attitude toward law, an attitude based on being human and loving. This same attitude contested tradition and the interpretation of the religious leaders of Judaism. No wonder they were shocked and alarmed. He spoke with authority and caused people to question and wonder. He had liberty not only to teach this attitude based on love of man, but had the boldness to live what he believed and taught. In a society bound to tradition and control such an attitude could only cause trouble. It is not without reason that Caiphas proclaimed that he must die for the sake of the nation (Jn 11:15).

Jesus and Worship

Jesus prayed and taught his disciples to express their need for their God. In his approach to worship, however, he downplayed the externals for the sake of the interior spirit. He says: "Not everyone who says to me, 'Lord, Lord' shall enter the kingdom of heaven, but he who does the will of my Father who is in heaven" (Mt 7:21); and tells us to be reconciled with our brother before we attempt to offer a gift at the altar (Mt 5:23-25). What is primary is not attending worship but how a man attends.

A similar attitude is present in his approach to sacred times and places. There is no sacred mountain where God is adored: there is no special time, but God is worshiped "in spirit and truth" (John 4:23). Man adores God in his heart and finds God where he finds spirit and truth, or in the meaning of the fourth gospel, where he finds Jesus himself, in his neighbor. Where worship abstracts from the life of man it is sterile and has no meaning.[6]

Jesus and Authority

Jesus faced religious and political authority and in the presence of such power he was also a free man. The scribes and Pharisees had the religious power and commanded respect. To them Jesus was a thorn since he would not allow himself to be compromised. He would not accept the system of the leaders and regarded their authority as nothing in comparison with the command of God. The system of religious authority arrogated to itself a power for the interpretation of the law which laid so hard a burden on the people, they could not sustain it. They forgot that God is freedom and not slavery. Jesus revolted against the perversion of the biblical message; God is not a tyrant; he is a good God. The leaders wanted to make God their prisoner. Jesus took God away from them and in liberating God from the control of men, he liberated man. It is important, however, to state that he did not deny religious authority; he placed religious authority in perspective: service to the good of the people in their relationship to God.

When he faced political authority he had a similar liberty. He was not afraid of Herod and acts in accord with his mission without worrying about political prudence; but he refuses to be implicated in a resistance to overthrow the power of Herod. He was zealous for Judaism but would not allow himself to be set up as political messiah; he would not allow himself to be king as a political force but yet he admitted he was a king. He could live with political authority but again would not allow such power to corrupt his mission. Certainly we cannot say that he liked the political scene but he could live with it provided it did not impede his mission.

Jesus and Social Pressures

Jesus was also free from the demands of society and family, which encourages a similar attitude. Luke tells us that at the age of twelve he placed his mission ahead of his family (Lk 2:49). The same idea is present in Luke 8:19-21 when he is told his mother and brothers are outside seeking him and he replies: "My mother and my brothers are those who hear the Word of God and do it." The episode in the synagogue at Nazareth witnesses to this same freedom. He was the son of a local carpenter but dared to stand in the presence of his townspeople and claim to fulfill an ancient prophecy (Lk 4:16-20).

His choice of friends was liberal in terms of social customs. He took meals with publicans, spoke with public sinners and accepted friendship based not on social demands and prestige, but on righteousness and faith. His criteria were always the same: the love of God as seen in the love of the neighbor. His life, his devotion, his associations as well as his teaching were free from social, political or religious control.

Jesus: His Mode of Life

And he was a prophet who lived with a biblical optimism as a celibate who found friends among the outcasts of society as he himself lived a celibate life.

The Pharisees reproached Jesus for speaking as a prophet and not living as a prophet and contrasted him with John (Mk 2:18-19; Mt 9:14-15; Lk 5:27-32). Jesus lived like anyone else: he ate and drank and enjoyed life. At Nazareth they were astonished that one of their own was a prophet, one who had lived among them as anyone else (Mk 6:1-4; Mt 13:54-58). During his preaching, the elite of society said that a prophet could not be such a common person; a prophet like other men is not worthy of credence and worse, he is dangerous because he disturbs the established order. The mode of life that Jesus adopted as the final prophet was a way of life in conformity with the people so that in the ordinary affairs of life he offered a religious meaning. We might think that miracles, which add so much to the authenticity of the prophet, should figure prominently in the life of Jesus while in truth, he often avoids the miraculous and does not wish that they be broadcasted. It is not always prestige that reveals God and so Jesus avoided the marvelous in his way of life (Mt 9:30; Mk 5:43; Lk 5:14). And in him there is a fundamental biblical optimism. Creation is good as people are good and God is good. The joy of life is not contrary to God. One cannot find in the gospels a basic sadness; the only sadness is the refusal of people to accept the joy that he brings. Nor can we say that he lived a miserable life. He was hard on the rich, even more so because of how money was used as a source of power. There is no great blessing to live in less human conditions but wealth is a temptation as a source of power and the kingdom of God will never progress in this way. To be poor does not mean lacking the necessities for a human level of life; to be poor is a relationship to other men. Jesus is poor but he does not preach only a simple rural way of life as an ideal to be striven for. What he renounces in his mode of life is the opaqueness of human relations which leaves an appetite for power of which money is the symbol.

There is one aspect of his life, however, which is quite different from his contemporaries: he chose to be celibate. Certainly his choice was not a depreciation of human love. You will find no words in the gospels that show even the slightest demeaning attitude toward women or marriage. He was certainly not afraid of women friends. Luke tells us that women followed him and took care of him and his disciples (Lk 8:2-3); he enjoyed the friendship of Martha and Mary (Jn 11:1ff) and was not afraid to speak to a woman in public (Jn 4:9). It was also his female friends who joined John at the foot of the cross (Mt 27:56; Mk 15:40; Lk 23:55; Jn 19:25-26). It would be unfaithful to the Bible in its appreciation of human sexuality and inaccurate in appreciation of Jesus Christ in the Bible if we did not recognize in these warm human relationships the need of the man to find complementarity in woman and the need of Jesus of Nazareth to experience in his person his own sexuality and his need for the support and understanding of the female. So his choice of celibacy came from his mission; the task of Jesus is not completely a personal task; he is the universal man. Even though all human love has a universal aim, it is a singular task because it is in virtue of the mediation of unique love that humanity is united. The task and responsibility of Jesus go beyond the concrete limitation in human individual love. Jesus aimed at a concrete acceptance of all that is human not in view of a terrestrial and historical possibility but giving the final meaning to all terrestrial and historical possibilities. A love which is singular and exclusive is tied to history. As Jesus was the one to give ultimate meaning to all of history he should not be involved in a singular love. This reason gains force if we consider Jesus as mediator. Human love is the normal mediation in the search for God. It is not without reason that the Bible uses the analogy of human love for the relationship between God and his people. But no one will be the mediator for Christ and his Father; he is the mediator. This is the exceptional situation since it is the only mediation which is the total mediation of existence inasmuch as it leads to death which is the completion of his celibacy. Christ as the mediator is the basis for his celibacy. Thus his celibacy, far from depreciating human love, paradoxically is the celebration of human love.[7]

The New Testament presents Jesus as a free man: free before man and before God. He is a prophet who lives an unusual life and points to the meaning of all of human life. He offered his fellow men a similar freedom based not on law but on his own approach to life, law, society and religion. He was a breath of life because in the name of God his Father and in the power of the Holy Spirit he interpreted and appraised the law, the scripture, from the view of love and thereby allowed devout people to remain human and free.

He stands above us all showing by his words and by his life that there is another way, there is a meaning to life that cannot be measured by prestige or power or wealth. The biblical Christ is real for in him life is real. With this as a background we can study further the biblical Christ.

NOTES

[1] Cf. Karl Rahner, "Exegesis and Biblical Theology," *Biblical vs. Dogmatic Theology,* (Baltimore: Helicon, 1964), pp. 31-66. Also, Edward Schillebeeckx, "Exegesis and Dogmatics and the Development of Dogma," in the same work.

[2] The recent development of redaction criticism in New Testament theology clarifies the different approaches to the gospel by the various evangelists. Cf. Joachim Rohde, *Rediscovering the Teaching of the Evangelists,* (Phila.: Westminster Press, 1969).

[3] The different Christological monographs can be seen by comparing such men as: Oscar Cullmann, *The Christology of the New Testament,* (Phila.: Westminster, 1964) who concentrates on the titles of Christ with Rudolph Bultmann, *Jesus and the Word,* (New York: Scribners, 1958), who takes a more anthropological approach to the experience of Jesus as seen in the New Testament.

[4] Cf. C. Duquoc, *Christologie,* (Paris: Editions du Cerf, 1968). The author is much indebted to this work for many of the ideas presented in this section as well as for the general approach of this book. See also, J. F. O'Grady, "The Attitudes of Jesus," *The Bible Today,* (Nov. 1970), pp. 86-92.

[5] Cf. Ernst Kasemann, *Jesus Means Freedom,* (Phila.: Westminster, 1969). Once again, the author is indebted to the provocative insights offered by this contemporary exegete.

[6] Cf. R. Bultmann, *The Gospel of John.* (Phila.: Westminster, 1971), pp. 190-91. Also, R. Schaackenburg, *The Gospel According to John,* (New York: Herder and Herder, 1968), pp. 436-439. The gospel of John knows only one commandment, the love of neighbor (Jn 15:12). In the fourth chapter of John the worship in spirit and truth is found where there is spirit and truth which in the fourth gospel is Jesus himself and Jesus is found where there is the love of the neighbor. Jesus makes the love of the neighbor the foundation for the possibility for the worship of God.

[7] It should be clear that the arguments for priestly celibacy cannot be identified with the arguments for the celibacy of Christ. Only Christ is the mediator and it is an abuse of language which transfers the prerogatives of Christ to the priest.

CHAPTER 2
THE JESUS OF HISTORY
AND THE CHRIST OF FAITH

Much of what has been written in the first chapter raises the issues of what precisely can be said of the historical figure known as Jesus Christ and how much of what is present in the New Testament is the result of the faith of the early church. Is there a difference between the Jesus of history and the Christ of faith? Before considering the more important questions and approaches of biblical Christology, something must be said of the "Search for the Historical Jesus."

For some hundred years the controversy of the historical Jesus has occupied the waking moments of many scripture and systematic theology scholars. For decades the quest was limited to Protestant theologians with the Roman Catholic theologians content to say that there is no difference between the Jesus of history and the Christ of faith. Roman Catholics generally set out to prove that the gospels were historical documents and so the picture presented of Jesus Christ in the gospel is the picture of the man who lived and died in Palestine in the first century. In the gospels, which are true historical and accurate documents, there were signs that Jesus was divine: he said that he was divine and proved this quality, especially by miracles and prophecies. The conclusion is very simple: there is no appreciable difference between the Jesus of history and the Christ we have come to profess in faith.

Recently, however, the Roman Catholic theologians have joined in the quest with the 1964 Instruction on the Historical

Truth of the Gospels,[1] and the Constitution on Revelation of
Vatican Council II. Today, most Roman Catholics readily
accept that Jesus, as seen in the gospels, is colored by the faith
of the early church so that it is possible to ask the question of
the difference between the Jesus of history and the Christ of
faith.

History of the Question

The search for the historical Jesus took its rise from the
autonomy of exegesis from dogmatic theology in the last century. Scripture scholars of that period centered their investigations only on what can be gleaned from the scriptures and tried
to develop a biography of the historical Jesus taken from the
gospels. This was a new emphasis in theology and scripture
since from the middle ages theology was more objective and
was interested in emphasizing the revelational aspect of the
mission of Jesus and seeing scripture in light of the findings of
theology. The modern approach centered on the consciousness
of Jesus and the internal development of his thought as seen
in the gospels in relationship to his mission. Often, then, there
was a desire to retrace his life with the abandonment of the
ancient dogmas of Christian faith.

Schlieremacher (1768-1834) was the first to lift the life of
Jesus to the level of theology in his work: *The Christian Faith*
(1821). He tried to write a life of Jesus without any reference
to dogma and considered the important element in such a
study was to bracket the doctrine of the incarnation and see the
life of Jesus as a human life in development as any human life
is in the process of development.

The work begun by Schlieremacher came to an abrupt end
toward the end of the nineteenth century when most exegetes
came to the conclusion that a strict biography of Jesus of
Nazareth was impossible. In 1873 the great Protestant theologian, Adolph Von Harnack (1851-1930) entitled his thesis on
the question: *Vita Jesu Scribi Nequit* [The Life of Jesus Cannot
Be Written]. The gospels are not biographies in the modern

sense of that word but are expressions of belief coming from the early community.

While scholars sought to write a biography, some also sought to establish a psychological portrait of Jesus. This effort had begun in the early nineteenth century with the publication of *The Life of Jesus* by K. A. Hase in 1829. There were others who followed this lead in the search for a psychological portrait of Jesus but they also came to a blind end with the growing assertion that the gospels were too influenced by the faith of the early community to establish exactly the psychological state of Jesus of Nazareth.

In the twentieth century the search continued with more and more emphasis on the gospels as expressions of the faith of the early community drawing more and more people into the whirlpool of doubt about the historical Jesus. If the gospels do not give us much information about Jesus as he was, how much of our faith is the result of the experience of the early believers and how much of that expression is dependent on the times of the believers rather than on the actual life of Jesus Christ? The responses to these questions are many and varied. It is not difficult to see how some could come to the conclusion that much of the divine aspect of Jesus Christ is the result of the early believers with an interpolation of Greek philosophy and Greek religions into the gospel portrait of Jesus of Nazareth.[2] The results of such influences are the doctrines of the Christian church about Jesus of Nazareth as seen in the early councils which have little to do with the actual historical Jesus.

After the first World War many European Protestant theologians centered their interests on faith as independent of the results of critical scholarship. The one individual who developed this thesis with repercussions that will resound for centuries was Rudolph Bultmann.[3]

Bultmann, a German Protestant theologian, became acutely aware during the First World War that for many of his countrymen and contemporaries Christianity and Christ had little meaning. He was steeped in German philosophy and well acquainted with the studies on the historical Jesus, and concerned with making Christ mean something today. With this pastoral intent, he began his critique of the language and style of the Bible and came to the conclusion that what is essential is faith and what we have in the Bible is a mythological interpretation of the experience of faith of the early church. If modern man is to come to an appreciation of Jesus he must go beyond the expression to discover something of the ever-present reality which is Christ. With this, the school of demythologizing was born.[4]

It is not easy to define what myth means to Bultmann. However, in general it can be said that a myth expresses a certain understanding of human existence, in the belief that the world and human life have their ground and their limits in a power that is beyond them. Myths give worldly objectivity to that which is unworldly.

For Bultmann and his followers there is an indestructible line between faith and history in the case of Jesus. Jesus is precisely that man for whom a purely scientific and phenomenological knowledge is insufficient. The evangelists recognized this insufficiency and have added their theological concepts to the picture of Jesus. These latter are limited and dependent on the cultural milieu and have expressive and practical value only in that milieu. The task of the modern exegete/theologian is to uncover the true meaning of the gospel which has been obscured by the ancient view of the world. The gospels do not come from the mystery that is Jesus but from the cultural ambit in which he was expressed. If we can get beyond this expression we can understand the meaning of Christ today.

The question immediately arises that if we demythologize the gospels we must place them in other myths which are in accord with our own understanding so in reality we are re-mythologizing rather than demythologizing. This the school of Bultmann will admit. They seek a new presentation and use as a criterion an anthropological approach, based, more often than not, on the philosophical anthropology of Martin Heidegger.[5] What may be asked is whether the myths of a contemporary philosophy are more adequate to expressing the mystery of Jesus Christ than the myths of first century Semites and Greeks.

What is of particular urgency in the message of Bultmann is the need to make Christianity relevant today. For Bultmann what Christianity preaches is that the Christ event is an event which summons man to faith today. Man responds by a decision to die to the world and to his sins and to live solely for God's Word and for the future which the Word makes present to him. No one can doubt the fruitful results of Bultmann's scholarship, even if today his followers are becoming more and more critical of the master.

Recently we have seen the rebirth of what we might call the new historical school. These scholars agree with Bultmann that the quest for a biography or psychology of Jesus is impossible and irrelevant, but insist that they are able to penetrate through the kerygma of the early church preaching to the Jesus who captured the interest and imagination of the disciples. For them, Bultmann was too quick to write off the gospels as creations of the early community without any possibility to reach the historical Jesus:

His action, the intention latent in it, the understanding of existence it implies and thus his selfhood can be encountered historically.[6]

There are still pieces of the Synoptic tradition which the historian has to acknowledge as authentic if he wishes to remain an historian at all . . . The exalted Lord has almost entirely swallowed up the image of the earthly Lord and yet the community maintains the identity of the exalted Lord with the earthly.[7]

Another follower of Bultmann to become critical of his master is H. Conzelmann.[8] For him, there are a number of elements which can be discerned in the gospels that refer to a unique unrepeatable situation in Jesus' own life and which cannot reflect any typical situation in the life of the post-Easter community, e.g., Jesus preached in a very limited Jewish milieu which was not true of the Greek culture. Hellenism was all around and it was present in his teaching. Also, it was different from Qumram. The followers of Jesus were not to rely on the false security of ascetic practices (Qumram and John). Their security was on faith in the God whose loving and forgiving attitude toward them was revealed in Jesus' own merciful words and works.

It seems clear that Jesus did appear as a prophet, a law-giver and wonder-worker and teacher: his words complement and reinforce his works and together constitute a meaningful and powerful encounter in the here and now with God as gracious and forgiving. He comes as the last summoner of all and proclaims the coming of the kingdom in such a way that it becomes real in his own gracious attitude toward the sick and the poor and sinners. In his humble submission to God's will he makes the future kingdom of God already proleptically present and prophetically alive.

The last name in the search for the historical Jesus should be Wolfhart Pannenberg.[9] He and his followers are new to the scene and hold that historical scholarship can arrive at the truth of Christian revelation. The dichotomy between secular and sacred history belongs to the past of Christian scholarship. For Pannenberg only the true believer can understand the meaning of history since the resurrection as the foundation of Christianity is the very consummation of history. For him as for many others there is no neutral Jesus of history, there is only the Christ of faith who is the Jesus of history and who calls for a response of faith. Either he is accepted by the man of faith in faith or he is just another man who has dotted human history.

Scholarship seems to have made a complete circle: from the acceptance of the gospels as completely historical to a denial of historicity as a result of the failure to develop a biography or psychological portrait of Christ, to a further denial of the historical aspects of the life of Jesus by Bultmann, now a return to the gospels as historical. This returning circle, however, should not be judged useless. In the process we have learned a great deal about the gospels and the Christ of our faith. Today we readily accept that the gospels are not biographies but are expressions of the faith experience of the early community based upon an historical appreciation of Jesus Christ, an important gain for Christian understanding.

To conclude, we can say that the problem of the historical Jesus is in reality the problem of history itself. The theologian and the man of faith must ask if it is possible to see in the daily events of the life of Jesus a condition like other men, something of the transcendent. Does the glory of the post resurrection Jesus have any anticipation in the daily life of Jesus? Is it possible to see something of the mystery of the divine and the mystery of Jesus in the life that was Jesus of Nazareth? The search for the historical Jesus is a real search for in the historical Jesus there was the presence of the divine, so says the Christ of faith. The two are not separated, rather one is the expression of the other; it is impossible to be words and not manifest in those words what is the reality. Without denying the historicity of Jesus or the influence of the faith of the early community on the gospels we can say that the Jesus of history is the Christ of faith.

NOTES

[1] "Instruction on the Historical Truth of the Gospels," Pontifical Biblical Commission, trans. *Catholic Biblical Quarterly*, Vol. 26 (1964), pp. 299-304.

[2] This is Bultmann's dilemma: "Does Jesus save me because he is the Son of God, or is he the Son of God because he saves me?" *Glauben und Verstehen*, (Tubingen: 1952), p. 252. Has the church made Jesus the Son of God because the believers needed to make him such?

[3] Cf. Rudolph Bultmann, *Jesus and the Word*, (New York: Scribners, 1958). This short book presents clearly and with much insight the fundamental Christological approach of Bultmann to Jesus.

[4] Writing on Bultmann and the demythologizing of his method is vast. For a succinct presentation, see Edwin M. Good, "The Meaning and Demythologization," *The Theology of Rudolph Bultmann*, (London: SCM Press, 1966). Or Ian Henderson, *Rudolph Bultmann*, (Richmond: John Knox Press, 1966).

[5] For a comparison between Bultmann and Heidegger see: John Macquarrie, *An Existentialist Theology: A Comparison of Heidegger and Bultmann*, (New York: Harper, 1965).

[6] J. M. Robinson, *A New Quest of the Historical Jesus*, (London: 1959), p. 105.

[7] Cf. Ernst Kasemann, *Essays in New Testament Themes*, (London: SCM Press, 1964), p. 213.

[8] Cf. H. Conzellman, "Jesus Christus" *Die Religion in Geschichte und Gegenwart, III*, (1950), pp. 648-51.

[9] Wolfhart Pannenberg, *Jesus-God and Man*, (Phila.: Westminster, 1968). In this book Pannenberg presents his complete Christology. For our purposes the chapter on the historicity of the resurrection, pp. 88-106, provides the basic approach to the question of the historical Jesus as seen in the gospels.

CHAPTER 3
JESUS, THE RISEN LORD

Christian people openly profess belief in a risen Lord. If such a statement is so important to Christianity that Paul said: "If Christ has not been raised, our preaching is void of content and your faith is empty" (1 Cor 15:14), then believers today must know what profession in the risen Lord means. As with every aspect of Christology, this expression of faith is a personal expression with as many nuances as there have been believers. With this as a proviso, we still ask what the risen Lord means to the body of believers.

Meaning of the Resurrection

To understand what the resurrection means demands an understanding of what the early church believed. Luke offers the early belief of the church in the speech by Peter at Pentecost: "God raised him up having loosed the pangs of death because it was not possible for him to be held by it" (Acts 2:24). Luke quotes an ancient prophecy and ends with the proclamation: "Let all the House of Israel know therefore assuredly that God has made him both Lord and Christ, this Jesus whom you crucified" (Acts 2:36).

Peter again speaks:

God raised him on the third day and made him manifest not to all the people but to us who were chosen by God as witnesses who ate and drank with him after he rose from the dead and he

27

commanded us to preach to the people and to testify that he is the one ordained by God to be judge of living and dead. (Acts 10:40-42)

For the early believers the resurrection of Jesus meant that he whom they had known and loved and had seen crucified was alive; he had been raised and this same crucified Jesus was now the Messiah in power, Lord and Christ, able to communicate his Spirit to others. By the resurrection Jesus had entered into his final and definitive mode of existence; the relationship to his Father was firmly and irrevocably established; his relationship to others was equally established in a final way. Now he was the Lord who could give his Spirit and make others sons of God as he was already the Son of God.[1]

The early church as seen in these passages was also clear in its belief that the work of the resurrection was the work of God the Father. He was raised by the Father with a definite purpose: to give his Spirit and to judge the living and the dead. There is no meaning to the resurrection without reference to the role of the Father and the corresponding communication of the Spirit.

The resurrection for the early believers, then, becomes the basis for faith and caused Paul to write: "If Christ had not been raised, our preaching is void of content and your faith is empty" (1 Cor 15:14). For all subsequent believers the resurrection is the first principle of faith in Jesus Christ. With this as the basis, we can examine the resurrection as the foundation of faith.

Resurrection as Basis of Faith

Today we are well acquainted with the supposition that the gospels and consequently the church as a community of believers grew from the Easter Faith of the Apostles.[2] Because of the resurrection the followers of Jesus believed in him as Lord and Messiah, alive and present with them. Other believers gathered with them in the presence of the risen Lord and es-

tablished the believing community from which the gospels and
other New Testament writings arose. Easter was the beginning
of proper faith on the part of the apostles and without Easter
there was no belief in the divinity of Christ or in his role as
the Messiah in power.

Certainly the gospels have formulae or expressions of faith
in which there is expressed belief in the divinity of Christ, but
these are de facto written in light of the resurrection experience
and thus cannot be presented in a direct historical line with the
life and experience of the historical Jesus. Expressions of faith
on the part of the apostles must be joined with the experience
of the Christian community after the resurrection. When the
gospel of Mark places on Peter the profession of faith in Jesus
as the Christ (Mk 8:30) or the gospel of Matthew offers the
same profession that Jesus is Son of the living God (Mt 16:16),
or Luke with his version: "the Messiah of God" (Lk 9:20)
each profession of faith must be seen in light of the Easter
experience. It is interesting to compare the variations of each
evangelist in this profession by Peter as it is interesting to compare the storm at sea: "Those who were in the boat showed
him reverence declaring, 'Beyond doubt you are the Son of
God'" (Mt 14:33), with "He got into the boat with them
and the wind died down" (Mk 6:51). Mark often seems to
record the events more closely attuned to the historical situation
while Matthew will more frequently see the same in the light
of the Easter faith and adds such phrases as the profession of
faith in Jesus as the Son of the living God.[3]

The Synoptic gospels are very cautious in attributing belief
in the messiahship or divinity of Christ to the ministry of
Jesus. This is not true for the gospel of John. This gospel shows
a greater development in the theology of the early community
with the disciples more often professing belief in the majesty
and dignity of Christ. In the first chapter of the gospel of John
alone, almost all of the titles attributed to Christ in all of the
gospels are offered by the apostles: Lamb of God, Rabbi
(teacher), Messiah, One who fulfills the Old Testament, Son
of God, King of Israel. In this chapter of John and in other
places (Jn 6:69; and 16:30) the disciples offered attestation

that Jesus was the Son of the Father. Throughout this gospel, Jesus frequently presents himself as one with the Father in a way far more daring than in the Synoptics: "Before Abraham came to be I am" (Jn 8:58). All such attestations and professions of faith are properly the expression of the faith of the early church and not the faith of the disciples during the ministry of Jesus. It was Easter that was the decisive moment of faith.[4]

If we assert that before the resurrection the disciples did not have full faith in Christ as the Son of the Living God, that is not to say that they did not have some faith in him as one sent by God in a special way. The faith of the disciples was a response to the revelation of God made to them which they recognized in Jesus. After the resurrection, the disciples could see the relationship of many of the events of the life of Christ which they had personally experienced and they saw how these manifested the truly divine mission of Jesus. In all probability, however, they could not understand this mission without the light of the risen Lord. If God raised Jesus from the dead then the death and the life of Jesus before this time must have been most important and thus all that happened in the life of Jesus ought to be considered. It was the resurrection that alone could give meaning to the life, as well as to the death.

We must say that the believers had to identify their faith in Christ with faith in Jesus the man or identify the raised and exalted Christ (Christ of faith) with the same Jesus of Nazareth (Jesus of History). The faith experience in the risen Lord drew attention to the historical life of Jesus which eventually was shared orally with other believers and became the basis of the scriptures. The disciples moved from the resurrection to an appreciation of the life of Christ which they then preached to others. No one should be surprised at such a phenomenon. It is quite usual that we understand greatness only when those who have that greatness are no longer alive, and then relate this greatness to others. As we read the gospels, the only thing we must see is that in his earthly life the disciples recognized in some sense the importance of this

Jesus of Nazareth. Certainly this must have been true if they were willing to follow him. As we have already seen, his attitudes toward law and religion caused people to pay attention to what he was saying and doing. His approach to sinners, to the poor, the way he prayed, his attitude toward God as Father, the preaching of the kingdom, and even his personal attitude toward his death as his life progressed, caused his followers to recognize that in this individual there was more than just a good man. Their experience of him became part of the questioning attitude that must have been present to his followers which would be perfected by the experience of the risen Lord.

With Easter and Easter faith the disciples could look back and see the major events of his life as manifestations of God; miracles, teaching, reactions to others—all were signs that God was working powerfully in Jesus of Nazareth. This is not to imply that all of these events were supernatural or divine activities; more than likely they were human events but much more than human events. With the Easter experience the disciples could see the meaning in these more-than-human events.

With regard to the Easter faith of the disciples we can conclude that this faith had its foundation in the earthly life of Jesus, but was perfected and understood only in the light of the resurrection. Faith in Jesus was very much like faith in any person. There was a fundamental intuition on the part of the disciples which grew to a fullness and complete acceptance. It was the experience of the risen Lord which brought this basic intuition to fruition. The resurrection was the first principle of the faith in Christ for the disciples.

Resurrection as Basis for Christology

As faith in Christ so also the understanding of faith in Christ must be based on the resurrection. Christology finds its foundation in the resurrection. To determine what the fundamental tenets of Christology are might cause some disagreement but certainly all will admit that it depends primarily on the resurrection.[5]

The primordial faith is expressed in the Acts of the Apostles:

He was delivered up by the set purpose and plan of God; you even made use of pagans to crucify and kill him. God freed him from death's bitter pangs, however, and raised him up again for it was impossible that death should keep its hold on him. (Acts 2:23-24)

There is a fundamental principle of New Testament theology that always connects the passion with the resurrection and sees them as aspects of the one mystery. This same notion is preserved in the primordial kerygma in 1 Corinthians:

Christ died for our sins in accordance with the Scriptures; that he was buried and, in accordance with the Scriptures, rose on the third day. (1 Cor 15:3-4)

Paul connects the meaning of Christ and his death and resurrection with its effect on us: "Jesus who was handed over to death for our sins and raised up for our justification" (Rom 4:25). The resurrection is the key for understanding faith in Jesus and in the light of this faith the disciples could reflect on its meaning and interpret theologically the teachings of Jesus as well as his actions. It is evident how the different evangelists interpreted theologically certain events in the life of Jesus in the light of the resurrection and especially is it evident that the meaning of the death of Christ was apparent only with the resurrection.

No doubt the resurrection must figure prominently in any understanding of Jesus Christ as it is the first principle of a biblical Christology and the first principle of faith. For the full understanding of Christ, however, the resurrection is not sufficient. The coming of the Spirit at Pentecost is a similar principle for Christology and faith. It is through the Spirit that we know God and through the Spirit alone we can call Jesus Lord: "No one can say Jesus is Lord, except in the Holy Spirit" (1 Cor 12:3).

Also, according to the New Testament, Jesus is the manifestation and revelation of God but not as absolute. We come to
know the Son and through the Son we know the Father. It
is only through the Father that we are able to accept the Son.
The same must also be said of the Spirit. Thus Jesus reveals
God and himself, and through himself, the Father and the Spirit.
Similarly, in Jesus God reveals himself and does so by the
communication of the Spirit in Jesus. There is no Christology
which is not trinitarian. The principle of biblical Christology
and of Christian faith is the revelation of God himself and
the revelation of God is made manifest after the resurrection
through the communication of the Spirit. God is revealed as
Father for us by the presence of his Son, made evident to us
through the Spirit. The first principle of faith for believers, as
well as for theology, must consist in the full event of the
resurrection of Jesus. This would include his passion and death
as culminating a life lived for God and for others; the resurrection as his exaltation as Messiah in power and the communication of the Spirit as sharing of his life with his believers.
This is made possible now through the glorious presence of the
risen Lord in his community, the church. With this as the basis,
believers turn with never-ending interest to the meaning of
Jesus Christ, seeking what the Spirit of God is saying today.
This is why St. Paul is so insistent that without the resurrection
our faith is empty (1 Cor 15:14).

The Resurrection as Historical

The literature on the historicity of the resurrection that has
appeared during the past several years has already become so
vast that few people can claim to have read and understood
all that has been said and printed. The issues are involved
and demand further investigation and research. What is more
important is the meaning of the resurrection as an historical
event.

At the outset we can say: the resurrection is a real event
involving the person of Jesus of Nazareth, affecting not only

himself but all subsequent history. But is it proper to call this event historical?

Many writers state clearly today that the resurrection is an historical event. Theologians and scripture scholars of all Christian churches give witness to this belief. W. Pannenberg, Protestant theologian, calls the resurrection an historical event,[6] and is satisfied that an historian using the usual methods of historical verification can investigate and establish the reality of the resurrection. Campenhauser, the teacher of Pannenberg at Heidelberg, writes similarly:

For all its contemporary, vivifying reality the resurrection is still an actual event of the historical past and as such it was handed down, proclaimed and believed. And so the proclamation of it cannot evade the historical question and cannot in any circumstances be withdrawn from the task of historical investigation.[7]

Raymond Brown [8] seems to be of the same school. He admits some value in the critical studies of the resurrection that have taken place recently, but seems to maintain a strict belief in the resurrection as an historical event. The list could go on with many theologians and scripture scholars differing in explanation or emphasis perhaps, but in general agreement that the resurrection is an historical event or can be seen as an object of historical investigation.

Other authors will take a different approach. In Romans 10:9 and 2 Corinthians 4:13, the resurrection is presented as an object of faith. If this is so, then can it be subject to the investigation of historians? An immediate response to this question cannot be given since it is not evident that what is an object of faith cannot be subject to historical investigation. Nor can it be solved by taking refuge in the declaration that the resurrection can be both. In the past certain critics of Christianity have discredited the resurrection of Jesus by prejudicing the result of historical investigation in the criteria used for historical verification. The historian, for example, can claim that for an event to be historical the following conditions must be verified: (1) the causality at work must be open to investigation; (2) reliable witnesses must be offered and not only those committed to the verification; (3) the event should have some analogy to events that are part of human experience. It is evident that under such conditions the resurrection is not an historical event. We have stated that the chief causality is God the Father and this we cannot examine and probe; the witnesses are friends of the one supposed to be raised and the resurrection bears no resemblance to what we have experienced. Others may minimize what is necessary for an event to be historical by equating what is historical with what has happened. "There is no justification for affirming the resurrection of Jesus to be an event that really happened if it cannot be affirmed historically as such." [9] But is something that has happened to be immediately described as historical? The presence of Christ in the Eucharist has great meaning and significance but is this an historical event? What does historical mean?

Historians deal with what has happened but precisely what has happened in time and space; the historian deals with what is localized and caught in time.[10] Is the resurrection an event in space and time? If it is not, then it is not historical. The very notion of the resurrection is that Jesus passed out of the empirical sphere of this world to a new mode of existence in another, the world of God. He moves outside the world of history, outside the ordinary datable, localized conditions of our experience to become the other world reality. The time in which our history takes place lasted for Christ up to the last minute when his dead body lay in the tomb, as still part of our world. The three days specify the last moments of his pre-risen existence, his last moments in human history. The resurrection meant that he entered a new mode of existence of the glorified Jesus, a pneumatic existence, a spirit-filled existence in which he is the source of life for mankind (2 Cor 3:17; 1 Cor 15:43).

Historians always deal with bodily existence under the ordinary time/space conditions of our world. The risen Lord does not belong to this mode of human existence. If, in fact, Christ as risen continued to live and exist under the bodily conditions which we experience and within which historians work, then he would not be risen Lord.

It might help if we compare the resurrection of Jesus with the raising of the daughter of Jarius, the son of the widow of

Naam and Lazarus. For the moment we can lay aside the historicity and historical accuracy of these events.[11] If we compare these restorations to life with the resurrection of Jesus there is a remarkable difference. In the three former cases the events are fully described while in the words of Ignatius of Antioch, the resurrection of Jesus took place "in the silence of God." In each case there is no difficulty in recognizing the three persons so restored to life while with Jesus there is a continual motif that the men who knew the earthly Jesus could not easily recognize him.[12] These are surely differences, but the main difference is that these people resumed ordinary life and no doubt died at some time in history. Their space/time life continued and they continued to create biographical details that some future biographer might unearth in an effort to record their personal history. They had not entered into their final and definitive state of existence. But for Jesus there was no return to life in space and time; his history was over; no more details would be added for his biographer; he had moved into his final and definitive state of existence and would never die again. The resurrection means that Jesus is not in history but has passed beyond history and out of reach of the study of historians.

To argue that the resurrection should not be accurately described as an historical event is not to assert that historical research and evidence are irrelevant. Nor would such a refusal to describe the resurrection as historical imply that the resurrection did not happen or was not real. The resurrection was a real event to the person of Jesus of Nazareth which would have historical implications for others.

We have already stated that the confession of the apostles is derived from and concerned with the resurrection of Jesus. This proclaiming faith can surely be investigated by historians and can be historically ascertained. Behind this confession lies the experience by the apostles that Jesus was risen and alive and had manifested himself to them and others on various occasions. Christ as risen Lord is connected to certain events of this world and to people who are part of this world. These experiences are historical from the position of those who experienced them but are not historical from the position of Christ. His glorified existence cannot be localized and thus cannot be dated for historians. Something similar can be found in the Old Testament. Yahweh is described as entering into history in regard to particular men and in particular times and places. But such occurrences do not make Yahweh's existence historical. He affected human history but did not become captured in space and time. What was and remains in space and time is the individual who has experienced the presence of Yahweh. Much the same could be said for the risen Lord. On his part, his appearances are not historical; from the part of the apostles and others who experienced his presence, the experience is historical.

History is concerned with the risen Lord in other ways as well. Even if we cannot reduce the resurrection to history, it would never have happened if there were not an historical Jesus, as the one who was crucified and then raised from the dead. The Christ who is raised is not totally disparate from the Jesus who lived and died.

Even if historical investigations have a certain relevance, it is at least inappropriate or inaccurate to describe the resurrection as an historical event. Much can be said for those who choose not to call it historical without in any way denying its reality. Perhaps it is much more accurate to refer to the resurrection of Jesus as a trans-historical event, an event in faith in which the believer accepts that the historical Jesus has already entered into his definitive mode of existence as risen Lord and Messiah in power; he has passed outside of the confines of space and time to be present to this world in his community and in the offering of the Eucharist. He is risen Lord who transcends history and by that meaning, is beyond the control of history and the search of historians.

The Empty Tomb

The controversy on the empty tomb reached heroic proportions when *Time* [13] magazine informed its readers that some Christian theologians were denying the reality of the empty tomb. As so frequently happens when scholarship reaches down to the weekly news magazine, something is lost in the process. When a theologian remarks: "It is ultimately a matter of indifference as to whether or not the bones of Jesus lie somewhere in Palestine," [14] explanations are needed.

The discussion on the empty tomb seems to have arisen not totally from scripture [15] but from theology with some influence from the desire to judge what has happened in the past according to the laws of nature and science as known to us today. Moving from philosophy and science into theology and then into scripture seems to have caused the controversy.

Anthropology and Christology are closely related; the more we understand ourselves the more we understand Christ and vice versa. It is a tenet of Christian faith that all believers and unbelievers will rise again. We believe in the resurrection of the body, but we do not know what this means. Recently, discussions in philosophy and science have caused some theologians to rethink the meaning of the resurrection of the body. If the human person is a unity composed of spiritual, physical and material elements, then what is death and what is resurrection? Karl Rahner offers his theory in *Theology of Death*.[16] For Rahner, there is no meaning in the separation of body and soul. Man is a unity and when he dies he dies as a totality. Nor can we speak of a human being without some relationship to matter. Influenced by Martin Heidegger, Rahner proposes a theory of a pan-cosmic relationship realized in death:

Since the spiritual soul is a real life-entelechy (though her powers extend far beyond that of giving life to the body, and despite the fact that the soul is essentially more individual then the entelechies of the sub-human realm), it becomes permissible to suppose, on the analogy of those sub-human entelechies, that the human spiritual soul will, in some way or other, maintain her relationship to the world. The human spiritual soul will become not a-cosmic but, if such a term may be used, "all-cosmic." [17]

The theory of Rahner is a good theory and quite satisfying. He maintains the fundamental unity of man and sees death as a broadening of human existence and offers an explanation of the resurrection of the body which finds acceptance in the scientific age. If this is a possible explanation of the meaning of the resurrection of the body for us, does this shed any light on the meaning of the resurrection of Jesus? If a pan-cosmic relationship is sufficient for all others, can the same be said of Jesus? If the response to this question is affirmative, then the meaning of the empty tomb is relativized.

One possible theory is that when Christ died and rose, he rose with a new relationship to God and to man and to the fullness of creation. His disciples came to believe in the reality of the present and risen Lord after experiencing that he was alive. Whether this was a bodily experience or a psychical experience is unimportant. It should be added that a psychological experience of the risen Lord is no less real than a bodily experience. (At times, a psychological presence is more real than a physical presence. For example, a person could be standing alongside of someone on a subway train and be totally unaware of this person though the physical presence was quite real. At the same time, this same person could be thinking of someone close to him, and that psychological presence would be far stronger, and he would be more aware of this person than the one he stood next to on the train.) Having experienced the risen Lord, the disciples preached that he had overcome death and that he was truly risen and alive as the Messiah in power. With such an explanation it can be added that later in the early history of the church there was a desire to explain this risen Lord and emphasize his living presence. From this desire grew the narratives concerning the empty tomb as present in the gospels. With such a theory the tomb need not be empty. Jesus died, was raised as the Lord in power, the followers came to believe in his powerful living presence through some religious experience of the risen Lord, preached the reality of the resurrection and later expressed this faith in the story of the empty tomb and the stories of his post resurrection appearances.

Such a theory has many good qualities, but alas many problems. The resurrection narratives are certainly late in composition in relationship to other sections of the gospels, but in reality they are quite early.[18] If the gospel of Mark is the earliest and can be dated in the early sixties and if an oral tradition is behind this gospel which is even prior to the separate sections of the gospel discovered by the form critics, then the narration of the resurrection, the empty tomb and the appearances are not too much separated in time from the death of Christ. The narratives were written early enough and emphasize the bodily aspect of the risen Lord: he ate with them, spent time with them. The evidence from scripture is too strong to be dismissed. It is easy enough to state that the faith of the contemporary believer would not be shaken by the discovery of the body of Christ, but "much more to the point is whether the faith of the eleven would have been shaken by such a discovery." [19]

What can be said of the empty tomb? It is a tradition that cannot be easily explained away especially since it is such a strong and early attestation in scripture. On the other hand, the content of faith is belief in the risen Lord and this may not necessarily mean an empty tomb. The Christian believer has always professed belief in the resurrection and this need not always imply an empty tomb.

The question of the empty tomb is in need of greater research and in no way is decided because some exegetes and theologians interpret the resurrection narratives as truly actual and bodily resurrection with an empty tomb. Nor can the question be decided because other exegetes and theologians interpret Paul in Corinthians to mean that he was concerned with the new creation through the resurrection and not a bodily resurrection and what the gospels witness is the firm belief in the risen Lord which is then expressed in stories concerning the empty tomb. In either case what is primary is faith in the risen Lord.

The Resurrection Appearances

The various appearances of Jesus in Galilee, Jerusalem, the problem of the many angels at the tomb or in the tomb, the chronology of events on Easter, the rolling of the stone, the earthquake—all point to discrepancies in the gospel narratives that no one can solve. Some have tried to relate the various appearances and circumstances surrounding the resurrection of Christ, but it would seem that such attempts are based on a faulty understanding of the gospels.

As far as basic reality and function are concerned, they all describe the same event. The gospels as we know them are not strict biographies or strict history. They were written and edited by men who tried to accomplish some set order, (and often a theological purpose in the background) of the various traditions about Jesus of Nazareth. That these men did not have absolute historical accuracy in the relation of these events makes little difference. The narratives are attestations of the faith of the early church which had come to believe in the risen Lord. There were men and women to whom he appeared after he had died; how or when or where or to whom really makes little difference. The sooner the Bible is viewed in this light, the more intelligible it becomes to the present and succeeding generations. The various narratives of the resurrection of Jesus can be accepted without any desire to reconcile what appears as discrepancies.

Finally, it may be asked, what does such a study really mean to the Christian of today? It means much. First, the resurrection must be intelligible to modern man and if a re-study of the resurrection will aid in this understanding, then the restudy is in order. The era of the apologetic is gone and in its place there must rise the era of a modern faith which sees the resurrection as an object of faith and the event which gives meaning to the life of Jesus, and as a result gives meaning to the life of the Christian. Because Jesus is risen he is able to share what he has gained; he is empowered to call us into a personal relationship to the Father; he is charged to give us his spirit, and it is only through that spirit that we can dare say, "Father".

Because the resurrection is the event by which Christ transcends space and time, the Eucharist is possible. Now he can use earthly elements, bread and wine, to be the symbol of himself and these elements can be the offer of Christ to us because he himself is no longer captured in space and time. Any explanation of the Eucharist must depend on an understanding of the mode of existence of Christ after his resurrection.

As he has risen, then also we shall rise. As he has now entered into his definitive state of intimate relationship to God, so we will enter into our definitive relationship to God. Christ, as the first born of many brothers, gives us the pledge of our own resurrection. As he has conquered death through his resurrection, our conquest of death is assured.

NOTES

[1] The gospel of John is very definite that the Spirit could not be given until Jesus had risen from the dead: "Here he was referring to the Spirit whom those that came to believe in him were to receive. There was, of course, no Spirit as yet since Jesus had not yet been glorified" (John 7:39).

[2] At first Roman Catholic theologians were slow to accept the remarks by Bultmann and others of "Easter Faith". Today this is readily accepted. Cf. W. Harrington, *Record of the Fulfillment: The New Testament* (Chicago: Prior Press, 1965), p. 95ff.

[3] Recently the redaction critics would offer definite reasons why Mark would have chosen to construct his gospel as he did, in particular his reluctance to have a profession of faith by the apostles before chapter 8, and then have misconceptions by the apostles after chapter 8 in regard to the meaning of Jesus. Cf. Willi Marxsen, *The Gospel of Mark* (New York: Abingdon Press, 1969). It is readily accepted these days that the various titles of Jesus as seen in the gospels are the result of a re-reading into the events by the early church. R. Fuller, *The Foundations of New Testament Christology* (London: Lutterworth, 1965).

[4] The gospel of John emphasizes the divinity of Christ almost to the point of docetism. It is the risen Lord who speaks to the community throughout the gospel. Cf. R. Schnackenburg, *The Gospel According to John.* (New York: Herder & Herder, 1968, pp. 19-25.) Also J. Plastaras, *The Witness of John,* (New York: Bruce Publishing Co., 1972), pp. 33-38.

[5] Cf. W. Pannenberg. *Jesus, God and Man,* (Phila.: Westminster, 1968), chapter 3.

[6] *Ibid.*, p. 88ff.

[7] H. F. Von Campenhauser, as quoted in S. Neill. *The Interpretation of the New Testament,* (London: Oxford University Press, 1964), p. 286.

[8] "The Resurrection and Biblical Criticism," *Commonweal,* Vol. 87 (1967), pp. 232-236.

[9] Pannenberg, p. 99.

[10] The author is much indebted in this section to the remarks made by G. G. O'Collins, "Is the Resurrection an Historical Event?" *Heythrop Journal,* Vol 8 (1967), pp. 381-387.

[11] The question of the reality of such events is heavily discussed. Certainly the raising of the daughter of Jarius or the widow's son could be cases of apparent death, or faith healing; Lazarus' restoration to life could be a construction on the part of the evangelist based on history, but not as accurately recorded. In any event the resurrection of Jesus is unlike any other and in each case the description by the early church makes evident that the early believers reacted differently to the resurrection of Jesus.

[12] Luke 24:13-35; John 20:15; 21:4.

[13] *Time,* Vol 86 (1965), December 10, pp. 96-97.

[14] Neville Clark, *Significance of the Message of the Resurrection,* (London: 1967), p. 97. "It is ultimately a matter of indifference as to whether or not the bones of Jesus lie somewhere in Palestine."

[15] Bultmann, *Kerygma and Myth,* (London: 1953), p. 41. He may have begun the study with his remarks: "The faith of Easter is just this—faith in the Word of preaching." This coupled with his demythologizing of the resurrection helped the re-examination of the meaning of the resurrection and the empty tomb.

[16] K. Rahner. *On the Theology of Death,* (New York: Herder and Herder, 1961).

[17] *Ibid.*, p. 29.

[18] Cf. Henry Wansbrough, "The Resurrection II," *The Way,* Vol 12 (1972) pp. 58-67 for a summary of the resurrection and appearance in the Synoptics. The author promises another article on the resurrection and appearance in John.

[19] *Commonweal,* p. 235.

CHAPTER 4
JESUS, THE PROPHET

To call Jesus Christ a prophet fails to do him justice since he is more than a prophet. Even if we limit the meaning of prophet to that which is present in Israel there is a limitation in the application of the title to Jesus since traditionally the Jewish prophets spoke the Word of God and we profess that Jesus not only spoke the Word of God, but was the Word of God incarnate. Yet he seems to have taken upon himself the quality and role of prophet in the tradition of Israel. As any title applied to Christ, it has its advantages and disadvantages.

The great advantage for us to use the title prophet for Jesus is that it emphasizes the man who spoke the Word of God and as man was the Word of God. Christianity has always risked the danger of confusing the human condition of revelation in Jesus with its radical source in the divine Word of God, and forgetting the human. To take seriously the title prophet guards against such confusion. Jesus as prophet invites thinking about the conditions for the possibility of revelation without any mystical exaggeration. After examining the biblical meaning of prophet as applied to Jesus, we will study the theological consequences of the human condition of his prophetic activity.

The Scriptural Meaning of Prophet

From what Jesus says and does, his contemporaries recognized him as a prophet: "Fear seized them all and they began to praise God. 'A great prophet has risen among us,' they said; and 'God has visited his people' " (Lk 7:16). "He is a prophet, equal to any of the prophets" (Mk 6:15). At first the reaction of the people flows from his miracles, but gradually there is a broadening of reasons for which the people recognize in him a prophet. The Samaritan woman accepts him as a prophet more for his authority than for his miracles. In the historical setting of his ministry, the people looked on him and saw him in light of the Old Testament prophets and in particular in relationship to the eschatological prophet who was to come.

Prophets in Israel: The Final Prophet

Prophets were part of the Jewish tradition for centuries with a profound expectation at the time of Christ of the return of the prophecy and the coming of the eschatological prophet. There had always been in Israel, both in its glorious age as well as its failure, a series of great men who spoke the Word of God; who announced the religious meaning that is present in life. The prophet rendered manifest the designs of God, proclaimed his judgment and revealed his mercy.[1] Israel had its heritage in which men and women could judge a situation and point out its meaning in the plan of God. The same people could evaluate an event and come to the conclusion that something was wrong. Moses saw the Exodus event as the great sign that God was present with his people. Amos judged his own times and concluded that there was something wrong with Israelitic society when the poor were oppressed. Both the judgment and the mercy of God were made evident in the words of the prophets.

What is important in Israelitic understanding of prophecy is the emphasis primarily on the present time. What does the Word of God say today? Is this a good event or an evil event? Are the people deserving of the mercy of God now or the judgment of God? Is God present or absent to this community? Frequently there was present some future aspect in the words of the prophets but this future element was dependent on the present. If Israel failed, then it would suffer: "Seek the Lord that you may live, lest he come upon the house of Joseph like a fire that shall consume with none to quench it" (Amos 5:6). A prophet was always someone concerned with the Word of God today.

At the time of Christ the prophets had been silent for many years. The law and the interpretation of scripture by the Scribes had taken over the function of the prophets of the past. However, in this silence there was a hope for the coming of the final and eschatological prophet who would issue in the last days.[2] "Then afterward I will pour out my spirit upon all mankind. Your sons and daughters shall prophecy" (Joel 2:28). The identity of this final prophet was not certain. Some thought it would be a return of Moses, or Henoch, or Elisha or Jeremiah (Mt 16:14; Mk 8:27ff; Lk 9:18ff). All believed there would be such a prophet and knew his specific function even if his identity was not certain.

The eschatological prophet would be the preacher of the final secrets, the restoration of the revelation to Moses; the last appeal to repentance, and he would restore the glory of Israel and destroy the enemies of the people.[3] To accomplish this there will be suffering, but in the end there will be favor for the people. "I will raise up for them a prophet like you [Moses] from among their kinsmen and will put my words in his mouth" (Dt 18:15). With this as a background it is easy to understand how the Jewish people would have looked to John the Baptizer as the eschatological prophet: " 'Are you the prophet?' 'No' he replied" (Jn 1:21). John was not the final prophet; such a role belonged to Jesus Christ.

Jesus explains the unbelief of the Nazarenes by appealing to his mission of prophecy (Mt 13:57) and in Luke (13:33) he remarks that it is not fitting for a prophet to die outside of Jerusalem. He never explicitly claims to be the final prophet, but does present himself as one who overthrows all false notions of God and proclaims "Repent for the kingdom of God is at hand" (Mt. 4:17). Jesus reveals, as the prophet, the final secret of the kingdom of God. It is not some esoteric knowledge; it is a communion. Jesus gives thanks to the Father because he has revealed this secret to the meek and humble, the little ones. The secret revealed is that Jesus lives as Son (Mt. 11:27). The Father has given all into his hands and in virtue of that shared life, he introduces men into the final secret and they can enter into a communion with God, the final secret of God and the coming of the Kingdom.

The life of Jesus of Nazareth assumes the recognized character of the prophets of Israel: he proclaimed the divine word and made the divine aspect of life emerge; he announced the secret of the kingdom as reciprocal communion between God and man and between man and the Father; the secret is the experience of Jesus himself. The message of Jesus could not be abstracted from his person and so his hearers ask him who he is. In response they perceive a radical unity between what he announces which is the kingdom of God and his personal experience. He manifests the final and complete sense, the mercy of God, which offers communion to believers and the judgment of God for those who refuse to accept this offer (Lk 10:21-22).

To call Jesus a prophet is good. The title emphasizes his revelational mission: the hidden world of God is opened to men in the words and events of the life of Jesus and all have access to this world through faith. This title does not exhaust the totality of his mission, but by emphasizing that it is as prophet that he reveals God as Father, we grow more aware of the humanity of Jesus who is like us in all things but sin (Heb 4:15).

Scripturally, the title prophet offers insights into Jesus of Nazareth; theologically it poses problems. It is the human Jesus who is the prophet. It does not suffice to say that Jesus is the eternal word in person to establish that the eternal word takes human form; the language of the prophet is human language and not the divine Word. What can be said of the knowledge of Jesus and his self-awareness? How does this fit into his mission? Jesus revealed God by all he did and said and so there must have been some knowledge of God expressed humanly, but exactly what type of knowledge? A theological interpretation of Jesus as prophet will respond to these questions.

Theology of Jesus as Prophet

The question of the knowledge of Jesus has been discussed for centuries, back to the earliest Christian times. From a glance at recent literature on the problem, the discussion will probably not end in the near future.[4] If contemporary theologians are at pains to resort to the scriptures we must then turn to the Bible and consider how scripture presents Jesus and his self-awareness. The solution to the question must involve the God who is revealed to us in the Bible, for it is this God whom Jesus reveals. If we attend to 1 Corinthians 2:8-16 and its allusion that man attains himself in self-knowledge and consciousness, and we are all conscious of the Spirit of God within us, then these notions must be applied to Jesus as well as to us: "The Spirit we have received is not the world's spirit, but God's Spirit, helping us to recognize the gifts he has given us" (1 Cor 2:12). We also admit for Jesus what Paul admits for all men: "All who are led by the Spirit of God are sons of God" (Rom 8:14). We do not hope to offer here a new solution to the problem of what Jesus knew. What we hope to offer is a basis for understanding. What is valid for Jesus is, in a certain sense, valid for us and vice versa. The question of the consciousness of Jesus and his knowledge is our problem as well. How can we know God as our Father, and the Son as our Savior and the Spirit as our sanctifier and defender, while living on this earth? How can we be aware that by the Spirit we are sons of God?

The Greek Theological Influence

The early Greek Fathers battled for centuries on the meaning of ignorance in Jesus. Even with the condemnation of the Apollonarians in 362 and the Council of Chalcedon in 451 which emphasized the true humanity of Jesus as well as the divinity, there were present those who ascribed to Jesus a totally divine knowledge, overlooking the human dimension. In the fourth and fifth centuries the majority of theologians of the school of Antioch admitted a true ignorance in Jesus, while the school of Alexandria held the opposite view. In the seventh century there is a new orientation. Maximus the Confessor refutes the arguments for any ignorance in Jesus and holds that for Jesus to assume our ignorance would be contrary to the divine dignity. After this, the majority of theologians had rejected any aspect of ignorance in Jesus. This theory continued throughout the centuries.

Augustine

Augustine proposed a similar thought on the knowledge of Jesus. He excludes all ignorance but not necessarily an exclusion of progress in human knowledge. Augustine, moreover, completes the Greek thought with the exclusion of any faith on the part of Christ. He possessed the beatific vision which precludes faith. As Jesus is the God man he has the dignity of God and this does not admit ignorance; he is the head of the church for all time and thus ought to be the doctor par excellence. These two reasons, the hypostatic union and the mission of Christ as head of the church, will be the foundation for all medieval theology of the knowledge of Christ, as well as the concern for the beatific vision.

Medieval Theology

The medieval scholastics and Thomas Aquinas in particular methodically organized these elements from earlier theologies into a systematic presentation which in turn became classical and influenced preaching and catechisms down into the twentieth century.

Thomas distinguished four stages of knowledge in Christ: divine knowledge and three types of human knowledge; beatific, infused and acquired. The two basic divisions of this knowledge flow from the twofold nature of Christ. Since the divine knowledge is proper to the divine person, Thomas develops more the threefold human knowledge.

The argument used by Thomas is soteriological: we are destined for the beatific vision; therefore, this vision should be present in Christ in a pre-eminent degree inasmuch as he is the cause of our salvation. "It was necessary that the beatific knowledge, which consists in the vision of God, should belong to Christ pre-eminently, since the cause ought always to be more efficacious than the effect." [5] A similar argument is made from the hypostatic union: Christ always experienced the blessedness or nearness of God. The basic principle used in this question of infused knowledge is the principle of perfection: if it is a perfection of man to have such knowledge, then Christ had to have such knowledge. As a result Christ received infused knowledge which was the fullness of perfection in the line of human knowledge. He knew all things.

Many of the medieval theologians would not admit any progress in the knowledge of Christ: he knew all things once for all. Thomas, however, admitted a progress in knowledge. How he explains this progress causes some difficulty inasmuch as by infused knowledge he already knew everything. In his presentation of the question Thomas develops his theory of knowledge as habit and knowledge in effect.[6] The difference is not easy to appreciate. Thus the medieval and classical position was clear: Jesus had the blessedness of the beatific vision, knew all things through infused knowledge and progressed in the expression of his knowledge. It is a coherent theological construct, but not very much in accord with the image of Christ in the gospels.

In the gospels Jesus appears with the cultural knowledge of his contemporaries; he poses questions, increases in age and wisdom (Mk 13:22); he prays to be delivered from his death (Lk 22:42; Mk 14:36; Mt 26:39) and is tempted (Mt 4:1ff; Mk 1:12-13; Lk 4:1ff). None of these descriptions fit in with the classical approach as we have seen. It is not surprising that modern theology, faithful to the gospels, detaches itself more and more from a construct that appears so arbitrary. Even on a less scholarly level, the picture of Jesus of Nazareth with his disappointments, his sufferings, abandonment by friends, uneasiness in the garden, and finally his death on Calvary accommodates itself poorly to the notion of absolute blessedness. A new approach is needed on the level of scholarship as well as the popular level.

Contemporary Theology

Medieval theology poses a rather simple approach to the knowledge of Christ. Once we admit the principle of perfection it seems sensible to recognize the solid foundations for the deduction of the qualities of knowledge and ascribe to him a complete knowledge. As we have already seen, however, this has little foundation in the gospels, especially the Synoptics. The research of the nineteenth century into the gospels and psychology of Christ demands a re-examination of the medieval opinion.

Perfection, in modern philosophy, does not consist in the static possession of qualities or privileges. Perfection is tied to autonomy and its acquisition; it is one's own personal activity by which one appropriates a quality or a value. To speak of perfection which is not personally acquired by autonomous activity or imminent development is not to speak of the perfection of a free agent, but the perfection of a thing. Knowledge which is personally acquired is an enrichment of the spirit.

If we apply these notions to Christ, the perfection of Jesus should be in the way of development and becoming. Infused knowledge which is not of the religious order, that is, not in relationship to his mission, is a theological invention with no foundation in scripture and offers little to Christ. The universal extension of this knowledge given to Christ in the medieval system by reason of his divinity is not in accord with the Son of God who is "like us in all things but sin" (Heb 4:15). Even if we consider Jesus as sovereign Lord, we know he accedes to this sovereignty only in the resurrection.

If the infused knowledge finds no scriptural foundation and offers little perfection to Jesus, what of the beatific vision? The co-existence of the beatific vision with incertitude, suffering, abandonment and the humble life of Jesus of Nazareth seems to be a contradiction. Passion and death accommodate themselves poorly to absolute blessedness. The conclusion from a more contemporary approach to the question of the knowledge of Jesus is that there is no need for infused knowledge and no need for a blessedness that is usually associated with the beatific vision. No doubt this theory offers many new possibilities, but they have to be more refined, especially in relationship to what has been said of Jesus as a prophet.

Systematic Presentation of Jesus as Prophet

Jesus is the prophet. He is the definitive revelation of the designs of God. He is the prophet in his humanity and it is in human language that he proclaims the saving plan of the Father. We have spoken of the function of Jesus the prophet as revealing the kingdom. The study of his preaching leads us to conclude that the object of his proclamation, the kingdom, is identified with the herald of the proclamation: Jesus is the coming of the kingdom of God. This causes one of the major difficulties in the whole reflection on the knowledge of Jesus.

It is not by chance that modern theologians are more attentive to the bond between the knowledge of Jesus and his consciousness. This never arose as a problem for the medieval theologians since they were not concerned with psychology and human consciousness. Since we cannot separate objective knowledge and subjective consciousness, the consciousness that Jesus has of himself enters into his prophetic proclamation.

One can easily understand the concern by some theologians and the official teaching of the church when thinkers begin to delve into a messianic consciousness and an awareness of divinity. We cannot reduce the preaching of Jesus to just another prophet. This prophet evidently considered himself as the presence of the kingdom of God: communion had been established between God and man in himself.

If we turn to the gospels there always appears the primordial importance of the subject. There is no full theory on the person Jesus of Nazareth, but there is a serious effort in the Synoptics to present the concrete human conditions. The gospels are not afraid to say that Jesus grew in wisdom and knowledge (Lk 2:52), that he did not know the time of the last day (Mk 13:32). Nor are the gospels afraid to condense into a literary structure the temptations of Jesus (Mt 4:1ff; Lk 4:1ff; Mk 1:11-12). As a consequence we cannot construct the knowledge of Jesus on a clear *a priori* principle: the absolute clear consciousness that Jesus had of his divine filiation. We study the knowledge of Jesus in relationship to the required prophetic knowledge in the condition of a servant in fulfilling his mission. Two elements are essential: the knowledge required to fulfill his mission and secondly, in accord with his servant condition. To bind together in theological reflection knowledge and consciousness is to risk representing the exaggerations of classical theology. To disassociate the two questions momentarily will facilitate the approach to the examination of what knowledge is necessary for Jesus to fulfill his mission.

To fulfill his mission Jesus needed a prophetic knowledge, but not infused knowledge. If he did not learn like his contemporaries, if he did not depend on others for language and ideas and expressions, then he was never like us in all things but sin. His prophetic function did not remove him from first century Palestine. To fulfill his mission he needed what might be called a prophetic intuition, a clairvoyance: an ability to bring the unity from the diversity of Judaism; a talent for transmitting in an unsuspected way the richness of the Jewish religion and its people. Such knowledge would not be acquired but would be a gift, similar to any such ability to see the unity in diversity and richness in the quality of life.

There is no need for Christ to have infused knowledge to accomplish his mission. He saved men by entering into the human condition with its obscurity; in this state he brought about the salvation of the world. Certainly Jesus had a universal love but this in no way required a universal knowledge. He accepted the limitations of the human condition imposed by

historicity and corporality and he transcended these very
limitations not by a transcendence of knowledge but a transcendence of love which is always the basis for any interpersonal
relationship. We will limit knowledge to the prophetic intuition
necessary for his mission.

The second part of our consideration from scripture emphasizes that Jesus came among us as a servant and in this
state he saved us. The immediate question that comes to mind
is the need for a beatific vision. Is it necessary that Jesus, for
his mission, as the revelation of God, possess an immediate
knowledge of that which he announced, and the possession of
the term of that announcement, the beatific vision? Many today
will insist on an immediate vision of God for the earthly Jesus,
but this is not the beatific vision.[7]

Christ, we have seen, is the greatest prophet, the revealer
of the Father. To be such a revelation he had to have a consciousness of the mystery of God. Traditionally, theologians
have identified this awareness of God to the beatific vision, but
if we concentrate on Jesus as prophet, there is no need for a
beatific vision. Jesus had to be present to God in immediacy,
but did not require the beatifying knowledge of vision as
understood in medieval theology. Moreover, if we take seriously
the servant condition of Jesus and the suffering and pain as
witnessed in the gospels, the scripture encourages us to deny
to Jesus what would be present only in the end of his earthly
life through the resurrection and not present during the earthly
life. To be redeemer, or to be God in man, the Son of God did
not have to assume a humanity in the state of fulfillment. In
spite of his unique awareness of his relationship to the Father,
as Son, Jesus did not have to enjoy on earth a vision whose
beatific quality would make his earthly suffering impossible and
whose total comprehension would make any increase in knowledge superfluous.[8] While on earth, Jesus was *in via,* on the
way to the Father, even as he revealed the Father. No doubt this
was in a unique way because he was the one who was leading us to salvation (Acts 3:15), but he was not one who
actually possessed on earth the full blessedness of his relationship to the Father. This was reserved for the glorious Christ.

We face the all-embracing mystery of the Son of God revealing the Father inasmuch as and only as he is a man.

Christ in his human existence possessed two orders of knowledge: a knowledge acquired in accord with his culture and times and a prophetic knowledge which enabled him to assume and fulfill his mission as revealer of the Father. The limit of that prophetic knowledge is defined by his mission and this as the humble servant of God who was the servant of all men. This last mentioned knowledge may be called infused knowledge but is in no sense the same as the classical theory of the all-knowing Christ.

Moreover, the mission of Christ does not seem to demand the beatific vision; rather it seems to demand that he not possess such a blessed awareness of God if he is to fulfill this mission in his humble condition. He certainly needed an awareness that he was God's Son, in intimate relationship with God, but this should not be equated with the classical theology of the beatific vision. One thing can certainly be said: the revelational function of Christ does not demand the intervention of a principal of perfection to understand the earthly condition of Jesus. Christ is like us in all things but sin; his perfection is in the order of holiness and not in the order of knowledge; nor is his perfection in any sense mythical or inhuman.

Throughout this discussion the question of personal consciousness of Christ has been lurking in the background. Interest in this particular area has greatly increased especially when it is joined to messianic consciousness or the awareness of his divinity. With the amount of words spoken and written on the subject, we may well be no closer to an answer today than before the discussion began. It is always disconcerting to hear the remark that Jesus was as surprised on Easter Sunday as his disciples. What can be said of his self-awareness especially in relationship to what scripture says of Jesus? [9] The scriptures present Jesus as aware of who he was, and in particular his closeness to God and his mission of revealing the final secret of God: the communion established between God and man in himself. We have already witnessed this throughout these pages. This awareness, however, could not be translated into the level of conceptualization or consciousness without development in time. Jesus always knew who he was, but just as we need time to express who we are, so he too developed in his self-awareness. There came a time when he could express in images and words who he was and this could not be before he had the ideas and the words to be used in the expression. If he did not know he was God's Son, the savior and final prophet of God, then he did things and said things that he did not understand. Such a position would make Jesus a schizophrenic. This awareness developed and was developing as long as he lived. In the development he was able to express his personality more and more clearly to others, and he himself became more clearly conscious of that same personality. He knew he was God's Son even if he could not always formulate this relationship to God. At what period of his life did this awareness first express itself? The gospels are not clear. The tradition of Luke 2:41-51 indicates that he was conscious of his unique relationship to God the Father many years before the theophany at the Jordan. His baptism by John cannot be an entirely new awareness of messianic dignity. As is true with so much of the disputed Christological questions, we will never know when he first expressed his awareness of Sonship. We can be sure that in the depths of his being he always knew who he was.

The question that can be asked is, "Why bother to go into such a thing as Jesus as prophet and knowledge and self-consciousness and awareness? Unless we are willing to be evangelized, we can forget the study of Jesus Christ; unless we are willing to see that Jesus as a prophet helps us to understand how we live our lives then we are wasting time and effort. As a prophet he was someone who could point out the religious dimension that is present or absent in human events and in a genuine way believers are called to point out the religious dimension that is present or absent in human events, or at least they should be willing to recognize it when others point out this dimension. We can talk about knowledge and self-awareness but how does that affect us? It affects us because it emphasizes how Jesus Christ was "like us in all things but sin." It would not be a tremendous help to live a human life if we have some ethereal God who masquerades as one of us, but it does help us to live a human life when we can believe that our God has become incarnate in such a way that he experienced what we experienced, that he was dependent upon others as far as his knowledge and his words and his ideas, and that he needed others to develop even his own ability to talk about his self-awareness and that, like us, he experienced the obscurity, the suffering or the pain which seems to be part of human life. We can believe in a God who is not disinterested in us and in how we live. That is why it is a good thing for us to think of Jesus Christ as a prophet for it should affect us in how we live our human, Christian lives. If we are willing to be evangelized, there is much evangelization that can take place. We see Christ in relationship to his mission, and give him what is necessary for that mission because it helps us to see ourselves in relationship to our mission and helps us to believe that we have what is necessary given to us to accomplish ours —that is Jesus the Prophet.

NOTES

[1] Cf. John L. McKenzie, *Dictionary of the Bible,* (Milwaukee: Bruce Publishing Co., 1965), pp. 694-699.

[2] Cf. Reginald Fuller, *Foundations of New Testament Christology,* (London: Lutterworth, 1965), pp. 46-47.

[3] Cf. C. Duquoc, *Christologie,* (Paris: Edition du Cerf, 1968), p. 134.

[4] Cf. E. Gutwenger, "The Problem of Christ's Knowledge," *Concilium,* Vol. 1 (1966), pp. 44-48. For a recent bibliography see: J. Ashton, "Theological Trends," *The Way,* Vol. 10 (1970), pp. 59-71.

[5] *Summa Theologica,* III, Q. 9, a. 2.

[6] *Ibid.,* III, Q. 12, a. 2.

[7] Cf. Karl Rahner, *Theological Investigations,* (Baltimore: Helicon Press, 1966), Vol. 5, p. 203ff.

[8] *Ibid.,* p. 205ff.

[9] *Ibid.,* p. 213.

CHAPTER 5
JESUS, THE SERVANT

It is of little help to ascribe every human perfection to Jesus. The tendency was not absent in the Middle Ages as theologians credited Jesus with a universal type of knowledge but did little to show how he was like us. His prophetic mission need not have given him an intellectual superiority; nor did he have to possess extraordinary gifts of nature. The New Testament assures us that he was very much like us when it tells us he became a servant.

Every since Harnack [1] in the last century, theologians have recognized the role of the Servant of Yahweh theme in the primitive christologies. The original title is found in Isaiah and carried into the New Testament in the gospels and epistles: "He emptied himself and took the form of a servant being born in the likeness of men" (Phil 2:7). The Synoptic gospels join the theme to the death of Christ and the gospel of John dramatizes the servant motif in the foot-washing in chapter 13 as well as in the death of Christ.

For the believer who wishes to be evangelized, the servant title has much to offer. We begin with the meaning of servant in Isaiah and in the New Testament and will conclude with the implications of servant or "kenotic" [2] theology today.

Four poems of Isaiah (42:1-4; 49:1-7; 50:4-11; 52:13-53:12) form the background of Jesus as servant. In these poems the author questions: "Why do the just suffer?" To his own question, Deutero-Isaiah responds that the suffering of the just, far from being absurd, is able to lead the sinner to repentance and ultimately to salvation. The persecution and pain of the Holy One of God is not without value. Somehow when the Servant of God assumes pain and suffering, he brings salvation to others. The response is clear, even if not entirely intelligible. How suffering brings salvation is left unanswered.

The fate of the servant is described in Isaiah, but the identity is unknown. Exegetes have discussed the Servant of God for centuries, holding at various times that the servant is an individual, such as Moses, or Elisha, and at other times offering a collectivity as the Servant of God.[3] In both cases the fundamental idea is that the covenant will be restored by the suffering of the just one for the people. He will be part of the people and will take on himself the sins of the people; he will be despised and will heal others:

He was spurned and avoided by men,
a man of suffering accustomed to infirmity,
One of those from whom men hide their faces,
spurned and we held him in no esteem.
Yet it was our infirmities that he bore,
our suffering that he endured,
while we thought of him as stricken,
as one smitten by God and afflicted.
But he was pierced for our offenses,
crushed for our sins.
Upon him was the chastisement that makes us whole,
by his stripes we were healed.   (Is 53:3-5)

In the gospels Jesus seems to have accepted for himself the title of servant. "I am among you as one who serves" (Lk 22:27). This same theme is present in the foot-washing in John 13. Mark states: "The Son of Man has not come to be served but to serve—to give his life in ransom for the many" (Mk 10:45). When the evangelists predict the passion of Jesus it can be viewed in light of the themes of the suffering servant:

He began to teach them that the Son of Man had to suffer much, be rejected by the elders, the chief priests, and the scribes, be put to death and rise three days later. (Mk 8:31)

He was teaching the disciples in this vein: "The Son of Man is going to be delivered into the hands of men who will put him to death; three days after his death he will rise." (Mk 9:31)

"We are on our way to Jerusalem, where the Son of Man will be handed over to the chief priests and the scribes. They will condemn him to death and hand him over to the Gentiles, who will mock him and spit at him, flog him, and finally kill him. But three days later he will rise." (Mk 10:33-34)

Jesus would be the Holy One of God who was rejected by men, despised and spit upon and through his sufferings he would bring salvation: "The Son of man has not come to be served but to serve, to give his life in ransom for the many" (Mk 10:45).

The same interpretation of the death of Christ and his lowly life is common in primitive Christianity as seen in the early professions of faith: "The God of Abraham, of Isaac, and of Jacob, the God of our fathers, has glorified his Servant Jesus . . ." (Acts 3:13).[4] Even when we consider the title of Kurios (Lord) in Paul, this title is earned in dying the death of a condemned man (Phil 2:6-11). Isaiah offers Paul an opportunity to relate the glory of Jesus as present in the risen Lord with the suffering of Jesus on the cross. There could never be a risen and glorified Lord for Paul apart from the lowly condition of the Son of man who died.

The writers of the New Testament apply the original meaning of the Servant of Yahweh to Jesus as a process of humiliation leading to exaltation. Death which is the supreme manifestation of the lowliness of the servant becomes victory as it issues in his glorification. The servant accepts the humiliation not as merely resignation to an unavoidable fate, but as submission to the will of God and the service of man in obedience. The servant freely takes on himself the sins of mankind and accepts death as the great sign of sin. By this dying in love and obedience to the Father, mankind shares in the glory of God. Throughout the New Testament the servant is one who obeys; God has the initiative and sustains the servant in his effort to bring liberation to all. This is the teaching of the New Testament even if the announcements of the suffering servant are reinterpreted in the light of "Easter Faith." The general theology is the same: by his death the Holy and Just One of God redeems man.

Further light on the meaning of servant in the gospels is found in relating the title to Son of man. Jesus seems to have used this title himself.[5] He is the transcendent one in Daniel who as Son of man does not base his power on his transcendence but on his service and the gift of his life for others. The powerful one who comes on the clouds brings a kingdom but unlike other kingdoms its authority is service: "Then men will see the Son of Man coming in the clouds with great power and glory" (Mk 13:26).

This title emphasizes the freedom by which the Servant accepts his death; he does not obey out of weakness but by choice:

"The Father loves me for this: that I lay down my life to take it up again. No one takes it from me; I lay it down freely. I have power to lay it down, and I have power to take it up again." (Jn 10:17-18)

The death of Jesus is the expression of his liberty and his love. The Son of man reveals his glory and power in the act by which he freely offers himself; this is his full emptying and his glory. The Son of man as Servant unto death has humbled himself but this is not degrading. The glory is present to Jesus because he manifests the goodness to God in giving his Son and the Son offers himself even to death for the sake of others:

He was known to be of human estate and it was thus that he humbled himself, obediently accepting even death, death on a cross! Because of this, God highly exalted him. (Phil 2:7-9)

This ancient Christian hymn praised Christ as Servant, emptied of the exercise of power that belongs to God:

Though he was in the form of God he did not deem equality with God something to be grasped at. Rather he emptied himself and took the form of servant being born in the likeness of men. (Phil 2:6-7)

He became one with us in our condition with all of its glories and its limitations and did so for love:

You are well acquainted with the love shown you by our Lord Jesus Christ; how for our sake he made himself poor though he was rich so that you might become rich by his poverty. (2 Cor 8:9)

The response to the emptying of the servant by the Father was the bestowal of the name above every name:

So that at Jesus' name every knee must bend in the heavens, on the earth, and under the earth, and every tongue proclaim to the glory of God the Father: Jesus Christ is Lord! (Phil 2:10-11)

The gospel of John offers further insights into the servant theme in the thirteenth chapter. Jesus, before he is to die as servant, expresses his oneness with his followers and his desire to offer himself in a helping way by the washing of the feet. It is no surprise that Oscar Cullmann [6] would relate this foot-washing to the Eucharist. In all three cases: the ceremonial foot-washing, the Eucharist and the passion and death, Jesus the Christ manifests his oneness with the human race and in particular with his followers and offers himself in service to all men. In the foot-washing he joins his followers in celebration as one with them and then dons the towel to wash their feet; in the Eucharist he joins his followers in a meal and offers himself to them in symbolic gesture of food and drink; in his passion and death he shares the lot of all men in death and offers his death as the culmination of his life for the salvation of men. The words of the fourth gospel make it clear that Jesus is one with his followers and they are one with him and in this context he can be their servant and calls them to serve each other:

He loves his own in the world and would show his love to them to the end. (Jn 13:1)

"If I do not wash you," Jesus answered, "you will have no

share in my heritage." (Jn 13:8)

"You address me as Teacher and Lord and fittingly enough for that is who I am. But if I washed your feet, I who am your Teacher and Lord, then you must wash each others' feet." (Jn 13:13-14)

Jesus is servant for his disciples but before he can be servant he has to become one with them. This is the same theme that was present in the hymn in Philippians.

From scripture we can draw some conclusions in regard to the meaning of servant. From Isaiah it is clear that the servant is beloved of God but very much part of the human race; he suffers as a just man with all of the sorrows of life and takes freely on himself the sins of others and in this serves them by bringing salvation. In Philippians Jesus is the Holy One who does not parade his divine prerogatives but empties himself to become like us and in his service to us to the point of death, brings the salvation promised. In John, the oneness with his followers and his acceptance of service for them are displayed in the washing of his feet. To be a servant demands that he who serves is one with those whom he serves with a free acceptance of the cost that the servantship expects.

Theological Interpretation of Jesus as Servant

Traditional theology seems to have been more interested in limiting the "emptying" of Jesus than in trying to understand what it means. This has caused great confusion with the result that most believers grew up with the understanding that Jesus was not a servant in any way that we could identify. In the thirteenth century Thomas Aquinas made a statement that should be the basis for any consideration of Jesus as Servant: "The truth of the incarnation demands this condition: human nature exists concretely in a humble state and not in a glorified state." [7] If the Word of God wished to be truly man then the Word had to assume the actual conditions of man which is far from glorious.

What is clear from Philippians is that the Word of God does assume this lowly condition freely; it was more than just an acceptance of a condition; it was not a revolt against glory or lowliness: it was a free acceptance of what it means to be human, an identification with us. We must also say that the acceptance of the human condition had a greater meaning for Christ than for us. He freely accepted our state; we are born into it.

Paul tells us that Jesus became sin for us:

For our sakes God made him who did not know sin, to be sin, so that in him we might become the very holiness of God. (2 Cor 5:21)

This is part of the emptying but this passage does not mean that Jesus committed sin:

It was fitting that we should have such a high priest: holy, inno- cent, undefiled, separated from sinners, higher than the heavens. (Heb 7:26)

"I shall not go on speaking to you longer; the Prince of this world is at hand. He has no hold on me." (Jn 14:30)

What it does mean is that Jesus accepted a humanity already tainted by sin and vowed to the full consequence of sin in death. He would be one with us even to the sharing of death with us. If he was to be a servant to us, united with us, then he had to accept our fate in death.

Jesus also accepted the ignorance that is part of our state. He did not, as we have seen, know everything, and was de- pendent on others for ideas and words and learned as painfully as we learn. This is nothing more than seeing the humanity of Jesus in the concrete. Some similarity is found here between Word of God as written and the Word of God as incarnate. In both cases the Word of God ceases to be absolute in its expres- sion. The Word is expressed humanly and is thus relativized. Because Jesus did not know everything, he could make mistakes and no doubt he did just that. As prophet he would not make a mistake in regard to his mission of revealing and saving; as servant his knowledge as a prophet was limited. No man has absolute knowledge; nor did Jesus.

The way one becomes fully human is through suffering and passions. It was normal for Jesus, as the Word of God as servant, to suffer. He had to suffer and experience the full play of intellect and passion and will. We may believe that since he was without sin, there was a harmony in Jesus, but we can never overlook the full sharing in our humanity. He was a man who experienced love and hatred, joy and sorrow, fear and boldness, hope and despair and anger. All are part of the human condition and must have been real for Christ if he accepted the human condition.

One last comment on the theology of the servant focuses attention on the point of emptying. In the past the emptying of the Word was seen as an internal process in the humanity of Christ as this humanity was possessed by the Word of God. Often enough theologians went beyond the data of scripture in limiting the emptying but refused to involve the divine in the process of servant. Certain theologians in the nineteenth century did not hesitate to transfer the "kenosis" to God himself so that the Word of God is the subject of the emptying. The Word of God renounced the relative attributes of God and preserved only the attributes of love and holiness and truth. The emptying is in the divine sphere with the consequence that Jesus was in no way conscious of his unique relationship to God his Father.

Such a theory was never readily accepted in Christian circles. It is unacceptable in faith and it is not necessary. A similar notion is found in the recent Death of God theology. The theologians of the nineteenth century were cautious in their conclusions and presented a certain ambiguity and incoherence. This is not true for the Death of God theology. The incarnation is a real symbol for the disappearance of God. There is no possibility for a relationship with the transcendent. With the incarnation the only transcendence is the transcendence of Jesus who is the man for others. The incarnation is the elimination of the absolute. The "kenosis" means that God

ceases to be recognized and honored as God. It is in encounter-
ing others that I accomplish the sense of Christianity. Thus
such theologians can speak of Christian atheism. The good
news is the announcement of the death of the old transcendent
God.[8]

Such affirmations are a bit strange for Christian theology
and now that the Death of God school has died, it might well
be dismissed. As is true for almost any effort to understand the
God/man relationship, there is something profound in this
affirmation, that should not be dismissed. Humanity is truly
the only sign of transcendence given to us. This sign, however,
need not be emptied of its reality. The disappearance of God
as absolute is the guarantee that humanity is the sign of transcendence which can be the only explanation for Matthew
25:40: "As often as you did this to the least of my brethren
you did it to me." These days, even the believer does not find
himself drawn to the beyond but feels the pull into the world
and the secular reality. We can also say that it is only here
below that we find justification. Salvation, as we shall see, begins
now. Jesus truly is the first one who announced that the
transcendent is exactly the universality which is made possible
by relationship to the neighbor. The "kenosis" of the Word of
God in Christ is the restoration of humanity itself, rendered
free by the servant who is Jesus.

It is not necessary however to proclaim atheism to maintain
this sense of "kenosis." It does not mean that God is suppressed
as absolute. It means that God in history does not present
himself under any other form than a fully human form. The
emptying is a process of the revelation of God. Because Jesus
was one with us then he could be a mediator and savior. He
was the servant of God, and the presence of God in human
history.

Conclusion

The title servant is used frequently in Christian circles today.
The church is the servant of the world; pope and bishops, and
priests and ministers are servants of the people; people are

servants of each other. The scriptural data and the theology of servant clarifies just how the title should be predicated by the church and believers today.

A servant after the fashion of Jesus Christ is not someone who condescends to serve; a servant is one who becomes a sharer with the one to be served and then freely accepts the demands and the costs of this service. If the church is the servant in the world then the church cannot be separated from the world but must become one with the world; nor can the church be so much one with the world that it loses its soul. The church, united with the world, freely accepts the sufferings that come from being a servant, one who heals, who does not seek to dominate, who arrogates no power to herself, who does not rely on money or economics or prestige, but as the community of the just, takes on itself the sins of the world and brings redemption, by serving in a lowly and menial way. Where there is need, the church is united with those in need and does all it can to alleviate these needs.

The same is true for the believer. No one can claim to be a follower of Jesus as servant without becoming part of those to whom he is sent to serve. Christianity is not offering people an opportunity to gain prestige by serving those less fortunate. Christianity calls the believer to accept his oneness with all mankind, and that includes those who are less fortunate and in need, to serve them by sharing what one has. The true servant is not above those he serves but is one with them. This is what the Spirit is saying to the churches today in an examination of Jesus the Servant. Believers can respond to the question posed by Jesus: "Who do you say I am?" (Mk 8:29) that Jesus is the Servant of God. To make such a profession of faith, however, demands the believer to be evangelized and become a servant like unto Jesus.

NOTES

[1] Cf. A Von Harnack, *What is Christianity?* (New York, Harper and Row, 1957), pp. 134-146.

[2] The Word "Kenotic" theology comes from the Greek word "kenosis" which is found in Philippians 2:7. Cf. P. Schoonenberg, *Concilium,* Vol 11 (1966), pp. 47-66.

[3] Cf. Oscar Cullmann, *The Christology of the New Testament,* (Phila.: Westminster, 1963), pp. 48-73.

[4] Cf. Acts 4:25; Phil 2:6-11; 1 Cor 15:3; Rom 5:10.

[5] Cf. H. E. Todt, *The Son of Man in the Synoptic Tradition.* (Phila.: Westminster, 1965), pp. 329-347.

[6] Cf. Oscar Cullman, *Early Christian Worship.* (London: SCM Press, 1953), pp. 105-110.

[7] *Summa Theologica,* III, q. 14, a, 1.

[8] The positions of Thomas Altizer and Paul Van Buren cannot be totally identified. For our purpose they are related sufficiently to briefly examine how their insights can help in the understanding of the "Kenosis" of the Word of God in Jesus. Cf. Thomas Altizer, *The Gospel of Christian Atheism,* (Phila.: Westminster Press, 1966), Paul Van Buren, *The Secular Meaning of the Gospel,* (New York: Macmillan, 1966).

CHAPTER 6
JESUS, THE SAVIOR

It is good to speak of salvation and redemption. We are all offered redemption and salvation through the coming of Christ. But what does it mean? Why did mankind need a savior and from what have we been saved? If we are redeemed, what difference does that make in our daily life? If Jesus has saved us from sin why is there so much evil in the world; why do people kill each other; why is there so much suffering and pain?

Some may reply that redemption and salvation are reserved for the coming world and the future kingdom. If this is so then to have a savior has little meaning for life as it is lived. People still suffer and sin and die. Salvation may be real but it does not affect people's lives now.

If believers cannot say precisely from what they have been redeemed and cannot speak about salvation as it affects human life today, then it might be better not to talk about redemption and salvation. The meaning of salvation and redemption in the Bible and in Christian tradition should offer some response to these questions.

The Need for Redemption

Genesis presents man with the possibility of living with others in peace and harmony with his God (Gen 1:26-31). The second chapter shows man and woman living in harmony until the entrance of evil in the world (Gen 2:23-24). If we try to discover the meaning of the fall of man in Genesis we

71

find a mirror in which we see our own reflection. These chapters were written during the tenth century before Christ in the time of Solomon. Israel was always tempted to deny her relationship to God by engaging in the false worship of her neighbors and seeking autonomy from God. The serpent represents the temptation to false worship: the tree of good and evil represents false autonomy. The possibility of peace and harmony was given by God but rejected by man. Genesis warns that if we seek autonomy from God and from the true worship we will find not life but death.[1]

Whether mankind ever actually lived with the acceptance of God and his neighbor is a mute question. We do not know if the first truly conscious human act was a rejection of God so that there never was a state of paradise. Genesis offers the thought that things might not have been so, even if they always were as we know them today.

The result of man's action is the power of sin in the world. Once sin entered it spread like wildfire until all was infected:

When the Lord saw how great was man's wickedness on earth and how no desire his heart conceived was ever anything but evil, he regretted that he had made man on the earth and his heart was grieved. (Gen 6:5-6)

Each man contributed to the power of evil by his personal sin until evil controlled all of creation. Genesis then narrates the story of the flood and concludes with the promise of God never again to destroy all life:

When the Lord smelt the sweet odour, he said to himself: "Never again will I doom the earth because of man, since the desires of man's heart are evil from the start; nor will I ever again strike down all living things as I have done." (Gen 8:21)

Times have not changed. The mirror that Genesis lifts up reveals that all seek autonomy and easily give in to false worship. Evil is present in creation; each person is born into a sinful world and has been contaminated by the evil that surrounds him. The contribution to the power of evil by personal sin makes matters worse. "All have sinned and are deprived of the glory of God" (Rom 3:23). Sin, the destruction of persons, is rampant among all people even among believers. Why do people tend to destroy each other? Why do we psychologically murder each other in small, subtle but powerful ways? People die psychologically every day, crushed by their fellow men. The power structure of business, of education, politics and even religion robs people of their personality and turns them into objects to be studied and places them in boxes for observation. Apathy and indifference contribute to our destruction. People contribute to the power of evil which takes its revenge in destroying them. Man was and is in need of redemption, in need of being liberated from the power of evil; in need of knowing and believing that the power of evil will be overcome and peace and harmony will be the victors to whom will belong the spoils of human life. Man was and is in need of the experience of salvation: an awareness that goodness and worth and dignity and peace are possible in the midst of what must be seen as an avalanche of sin and evil and death and destruction. We all need to be saved from being alone and selfish and bent on self-destruction and the destruction of others; all need to believe in a future for mankind and his planet that is good in which there will be the final triumph of what is noble and true. Jesus brings all of this to us.

Redemption [2]

The New Testament shows a marked lack of interest in this particular word. It is found principally in the Old Testament and refers to the "buying back" of the first born dedicated to Yahweh (Ex 34:20; Num 18:15). Later it refers to the action of God in redeeming Israel from the slavery of Egypt (Dt 7:8; 24:18). In the later writings it is transferred to the individual who is redeemed in the sense of liberation (Jer 15:21; 2 Sam 4:9).

The writers of the New Testament continue the use as found in the Old Testament, but with greater emphasis on the aspect of liberation. The implication of ransom is almost never found except perhaps in Mk 10:45 and Mt 20:28. Even in these passages there is not necessarily a connotation of "buying back." [3] It seems to be near the truth to say that "redemption" was not one of the major ways in which the early church described the work of Jesus. For our purposes we can state that it fundamentally connotes a liberation from sin, the "principalities and powers," the law and death (Rom 3:24; 1 Cor 1:30; Eph 1:7; Col 1:14; Heb 9:15). The one additional note from the New Testament congruent for the discussion here is the universality of the redemption. Jesus died and rose for all men and liberated all men from the power of evil and sin and death (Phil 3:10; Rom 4:25; 1 Cor 6:14; 2 Cor 4:14). Redemption is liberation for all.

The redemption is also the sole work of Christ who by his death has freed us. He was the servant of God who was united with us to serve and offer himself for us (Mk 10:45; Mt 20:28; Jn 13:1). By his death we have been freed from sin (Tit 2:14; Eph 1:7; Col 1:14), freed from the law (Gal 3:13; Rom 7:1ff) and have been given a new birth and new creation (2 Cor 5:17), have been justified (Rom 5:1), granted the Spirit of God by which we are children of God (Gal 3:2ff; Rom 8:12-17), and are filled with truth and light and joy and peace. When we move from the meaning of redemption as "liberation" to the experience of redemption, we move to the meaning of "salvation" in the New Testament.

Salvation [4] in the Bible is far more important than the word redemption. Jesus preaches salvation by the proclamation of the kingdom of God. With him there is a communion established between God and man which is the meaning of being saved. The gospel is the message of salvation (Acts 13:26), the way of salvation (Acts 16:17), and the power of God for salvation (Rom 1:16).

The content of "salvation" offers a wealth of ideas. Present salvation is created for all by the death of Jesus with its liberation from law and sin (Rom 6:1ff; 1 Tim 1:15; Eph 2:1-10); divine Sonship is offered (Rom 8:14-17); people are justified by grace (Rom 3:24). As with redemption it is present and yet to come (Heb 9:28; Rom 8:24; Phil 3:20).

Redemption and salvation, evidently, are closely related terms in the Bible. This juxtaposition of terms has prompted us to use the terms interchangeably in history. For purposes of understanding and education it seems better to distinguish the terms while not separating them. Redemption emphasizes that good will win out and evil will eventually be overcome because of the coming of Jesus. Even now the kingdom is made present and manifest in him; there is a communion established between God and man and between man and man. Evil and selfishness cannot overcome totally the fundamental sense of goodness and unity that man has as a possibility. To be redeemed offers us the assurance that good has already triumphed.

Salvation emphasizes the actual experience of peace and harmony and truth and goodness that is given to us by the redemptive death of Christ. Jesus not only offers a future triumph of good, but he brings the experience of this future to the present. Even with this understanding, however, we still face the question: What effect does salvation have on individual lives now?

Salvation: The Experience of Redemption

Negative approaches have their merit. To try to understand salvation we begin with an examination of its opposite: damnation. When we have identified with the experience of damnation we might be able to discover the place of salvation.

Damnation is a powerful word; it is also part of everyday experience. Alienation is also a powerful word and equally a part of everyday experience. Both words are hackneyed expressions lacking in clarity. Alienation connotes apathy and rebellion, conformity and deviance, social isolation. Damnation connotes fire and brimstone and eternity and suffering and pain. People use alienation but do not take time to define it; others use damnation and pose it as a threat with an equal lack of effort to explain. Both ideas are related. The modern experience of alienation fits closely the classical meaning of damnation and it is from both that Jesus saves.

Everyone experiences damnation and alienation in life. There are times when we say: "Why bother? It is just not worth the effort." We try very hard and things just do not work out; evil seems to prosper and the good tend to come in last. There are times when we all feel sorry for ourselves, mad at the world and interested only in ourselves. Each is the experience of alienation and damnation and it is real for all of us.

Alienation in psychology can be divided into six distinct but related categories, each a part of human experience.[5] Such analysis helps us to understand the meaning of damnation:

Individual Powerlessness

No one has any control over his own life; we are unable to decide our future since destiny is in the hands of some dark external force such as luck or fate or the government. We all feel this way at times; no power, no possibility of doing anything with life; we feel as though we are being manipulated by some strange force.

Meaninglessness

Life is absurd, incomprehensible. Nothing seems to make sense. Society will never change. No one understands how or why things happen. This is the experience of "Why bother? It doesn't make any sense and perhaps it never will."

Normlessness (Cynicism)

Normal methods do not work. Cheating and cutting corners are the only way to get ahead. Hard work and honesty do not pay. The good always finish last. People, events and values are not to be trusted.

Cultural Estrangement

Something is wrong with the way we are living. Those who set up the standards of life must be insane. Pity those who have to grow up in this country. The values have been lost.

Self-Estrangement

The individual is painfully aware of the difference between the ideal self and the real self, and it is not always encouraging. We do not live up to what we believe: we are not all we ought to be.

Social Isolation

Life is lonely—we live separated lives. Everyone is on a periphery of existence at times; there is a sadness that permeates all of life and no one seems to be able to overcome its pervasiveness.

Alienation is much more than a set of attitudes but runs deep into the total human personality affecting and influencing the spiritual as well as the psychological and the physical. Most of us can identify with these feelings at some time or other; they are part of the human scene. Yet we can also realize that if such feelings are dominant and take over the major part of a person's life, that person is far from living a human life and theologically we can say that that person is experiencing damnation. It is from this that Jesus redeems.

Redemption, as has been said, is the sure belief that good will win out and that evil will eventually be overcome, even as we continue to experience the power of evil and sin. Jesus redeems us from hopelessness. We will go back and compare with the attitudes of alienation:

Individual Powerlessness

Mankind's future is not in the hands of some dark external force or fate or the government. We are not manipulated by

some power, but are assured that the power that controls life
is good and interested in us, and gives the possibility of doing
something with our lives. Even as we experience periods of
powerlessness, Jesus assures us that it is not so:

We know that God makes all things work together for the good
of those who have been called according to his decree. Those
whom he foreknew he predestined to share the image of his
Son, that the Son might be the first-born of many brothers.
Those he predestined he likewise called; those he called he also
justified; and those he justified he in turn glorified. (Rom 8:28-32)

Meaninglessness

Life is not absurd; life has meaning. Jesus tells us this and
shows us by his life that he lived for others. There is always a
purpose in life if we have the courage to live for others. We
may never change the world, but we can always change ourselves and we can find meaning in the way that Jesus lived and
calls us to live:

"All this I tell you that my joy may be yours and your joy may
be complete. This is my commandment: love one another as I
have loved you." (Jn 15:11-13)

Normlessness (Cynicism)

Perhaps it appears as if hard work and honesty do not
succeed but looks can be deceiving. It may appear that Christians are losers but they are not; they can find themselves at
peace and can achieve some harmony in the world. It will work
because Jesus has promised that there will be a good future:

"I tell you all this that in me you may find peace, you will suffer
in the world. But take courage! I have overcome the world."
(Jn 16:33)

Cultural Estrangement

There are values present in life even if they are not always
accepted. Jesus redeems us from failure to see the possibili-

ties that are present in every human life. As long as there is life, there is a fundamental value which is the foundation of that life:

Praised be the God and Father of our Lord Jesus Christ, who has bestowed on us in Christ every spiritual blessing in the heavens! God chose us in him before the world began, to be holy and blameless in his sight, to be full of love; he likewise predestined us through Christ Jesus to be his adopted sons—such was his will and pleasure—that all might praise the glorious favor he has bestowed on us in his beloved. (Eph 1:3-6)

Self-Estrangement

No one lives up to what he would like. Jesus redeems us from our own failure by telling us that in spite of that failure we have value in the sight of God our Father. There is always a new possibility that we can be more than we are at the moment: we can always bring good to the fore and come closer to living the way we would like and we have the reassurance that in spite of failure and sin we are still precious in his eyes and in the eyes of his church:

"Look at the birds in the sky. They do not sow or reap, they gather nothing into barns; yet your heavenly Father feeds them. Are not you more important than they?" (Mt 6:26)

"Seek first his kingship over you, his way of holiness, and all these things will be given you besides." (Mt 6:33)

Social Isolation

Jesus is our friend and he gives us his friends: "You are my friends if you do what I command you" (Jn 15:14). We need never feel totally isolated since Jesus redeems us from the aloneness and isolation and offers companionship.

Then Jesus looked at love and told him, "There is one more thing that you must do. Go and sell what you have and give to the poor; you will then have treasure in heaven." (Mk 10:21)

Jesus liberates us from damnation, from alienation, and offers a new possibility to each of us. We easily identify with the experience of damnation and faith assures us that this need not be so. We are just and freed from sin and law and are God's household. We need to experience salvation stronger than we need to experience damnation.

Salvation

Scripture speaks of redemption but infrequently: it is more interested in the effects of redemption, the experience of salvation. There cannot be redemption which is not part of life. If we experience damnation and contribute to each other's damnation, the same is true for salvation. It is present and real for everyone.

Salvation is the experience of the peace and harmony and good will that comes in those moments of life when all seems good. Jesus redeems from the control of the negative and sin, and offers the experience of this future reality in the present. Salvation is NOW.

Several years ago Karl Rahner was giving a lecture in Rome on salvation and remarked that salvation "is a bottle of coke." [6] All over Europe there are signs: "Things go better with Coke." Rahner described the experience: "The day is hot and the streets of Rome are dusty and filled with exhaust from the buses; you walk along with your friend, you see the sign, sit down and enjoy the comfort and ease of a bottle of coke with your friend. Salvation is a bottle of coke." [7] Whatever contributes to the well-being of mankind, whatever is good and lovely and noble and true is the experience of salvation. Salvation is not reserved for the future alone. It is present when a family sits down at a family celebration and enjoys each other's company in thanksgiving for the goodness they have received and the goodness they contribute to each other and enjoy fine food and good wine and great company. Salvation is experienced by a walk in an autumn rain when all of a sudden there is a freshness present in the world. Or salvation is experienced in the love that exists between husband and wife, parents and children. Salvation is present when we go out of our way to contribute to the goodness of others. It is mediated to us when we graciously accept the kindness of someone who is thoughtful enough to send a birthday card, or bring a gift, or send flowers or write a thank you note, or anything at all that makes a better person. Anything that makes people more aware of the goodness of God and the goodness that is present in creation and the goodness that is present in other people's lives and one's personal life is the awareness of salvation. If man did not have these experiences he would be on the brink of despair. There must be some movements in life when we are aware of a possibility for peace; when there is a possibility for people blessing each other's goodness instead of so frequently condemning each other's evils and wrongdoings. If we did not at times experience the value and worth in being alive, there would be little enthusiasm for life. It is only the experience of salvation that can redeem the efforts we must make if we are to bring this salvation to others. Salvation has to be real, otherwise it is a beautiful doctrine which does not mean anything as far as our lives are concerned. Unless we are able to move out of selfishness and feeling sorry for ourselves and contribute to the good of someone else, then we are not believers, we are not saved.

It is a simple thing to say that Jesus redeems us and saves us, but there is a richness that does not come through in the words. Jesus redeems us from the power of evil and sin and gives us the concrete experience of the peace and harmony for which we all long. People too easily contribute to each other's damnation instead of salvation. Damnation and alienation spread farther and quicker than salvation. If Christianity means anything, if profession of belief in Jesus as savior makes sense, then every believer should be interested in experiencing more and more salvation and be interested in helping others experience the same. The power of evil in this world should be lessening through the power of good people. This is not an easy task; Jesus never said that it would be. He assures us that: "In the world you will have trouble, but be of good cheer, I have overcome the world" (Jn 16:33). Salvation is as real as we will make Jesus of Nazareth and what a delightful life it would be if believers could increase the moments of salvation and delete the experience of damnation.

Throughout this chapter the emphasis has been on salvation as experienced NOW. The intent was to overcome a previous emphasis in Christian tradition which reserved redemption and salvation for the future life. If salvation and redemption are real they have to affect the lives that people live now. But salvation is not complete; the full power of the redemption is not yet made evident; there is much that is present in life as a result of the coming of Jesus of Nazareth and there is much that is to come. We await the day that is to come where there will be a new heaven and a new earth:

Then I saw new heavens and a new earth. The former heavens and the former earth had passed away and the sea was no longer. I also saw a new Jerusalem, the holy city, coming down out of heaven from God, beautiful as a bride prepared to meet her husband. I heard a loud voice from the throne cry out: "This is God's dwelling among men. He shall dwell with them and they shall be his people and he shall be their God who is always with them. He shall wipe every tear from their eyes, and there shall be no more death or mourning, crying out or pain for the former world has passed away." (Rev 21:1-4)

Jesus is redeemer and savior.

NOTES

[1] It is not possible to develop a complete exegesis of Genesis in these pages. Cf. A Sulezer, *The Pentateuch*, (New York: Herder and Herder, 1964), pp. 24-32; J. Plastaras, *Creation and Covenant*, (Milwaukee: Bruce Publishing Co., 1968), pp. 36-64.

[2] Standard Dictionaries of the Bible offer sufficient coverage of these ideas. Cf. John L. McKenzie, *Dictionary of the Bible*, (Milwaukee: Bruce Publishing Co., 1965); L. Hartman, *Encyclopedic Dictionary of the Bible*. (New York: McGraw-Hill, 1963).

[3] The concept of "buying back" figured prominently in medieval

theology with the additional notion that mankind was bought back from Satan by the redemption of Christ. Cf. Boniface A. Willems, *The Reality of the Redemption.* (New York: Herder and Herder, 1970), pp. 49-60.

[4] Cf. "Salvation," *Sacramentum Mundi,* Vol 5 (New York: Herder and Herder, 1970).

[5] This division is taken from: Melvin Seeman, "Alienation, A Map." *Psychology Today,* Vol 5 (1971), pp. 83-84.

[6] These remarks are taken from notes prepared from tapes of the lectures. For a fuller presentation, Cf.: "Salvation," *Sacramentum Mundi,* Vol. 6.

[7] *Ibid.*

CHAPTER 7
JESUS, THE WORD OF GOD

Jesus of Nazareth has a certain universality even as he is an individual of first century Palestine. His appeal and lasting influence are based on more than just his teaching. This poses the question: "What is the bond between the Word he offers and the being that he is?" In the gospel of John the author is not afraid to say that "The Word became flesh" in Jesus the Christ.

Today we tend to take it for granted that the Word of God became flesh in Jesus but how can it be possible to join an eternal Word with an incarnate Word? How is the infinite expressed within the finite? And God with man? The originality of Christianity as a religion joins the eternal Word of God in an historical personage. Jesus is not just another prophet. The prophet gives testimony to the Word of God; he effaces himself and matters little. But Jesus is the eschatological prophet; he does not have the Word of God addressed to himself; he is the Word of God who speaks on his own authority. The office of revealing God is based not on a vocation to bear the Word of God, but on the identification between bearer and what is born.

We must understand the meaning of the Word of God in scripture and then make application to Jesus and finally application to individual believers who learn about themselves by listening to the Word of God.

The Biblical Meaning of Word

Jesus is identified with the Word of God only in the fourth gospel, chapter 1, and in the Apocalypse (19:13). All admit

85

this. Such a restricted use of the term does not mean, however, that the other New Testament writings do not see the relation between Jesus and the Word of God. The Acts of the Apostles and the epistles rarely mention the words of Jesus and the Synoptics make no effort to report all the words of Jesus. The primitive community did not profess a superstitious cult of the words of Jesus since his words did not constitute a reality separated from Jesus himself. Because Jesus was the Word of God the actual words he used were not considered of greatest import.[1] It was the life of Jesus as lived and his death and resurrection which were preached as the Word of God. The Acts of the Apostles identified the Word of God with the good news of Jesus Christ in the early preaching. "The Word of God continued to spread, while at the same time the number of disciples in Jerusalem increased enormously" (Acts 6:7). Jesus is not identified as the Word of God but there is no Word of God apart from Jesus.

Paul used the word gospel to express the Christian message and at times refers to the word of truth (Eph 1:13) and the word of Christ (Col 3:16) but, like the Acts, does not identify the Word of God with Jesus. Outside of the Johannine writings there exists a theology of the Word of God in virtue of its object, Jesus, which will orient us to understand the fourth gospel. For Paul and the Synoptics Jesus is the Word of God because he expresses the saving designs of God and fulfills the prophetic revelation, a clearly functional approach.

John alone presents Jesus as the Word who enjoys a role before creation and the Word become flesh. To understand the Johannine use demands an understanding of the meaning of Word in the Old Testament.

Traditionally the Hebrew word "dabar" has a double role; it is the dynamic creative power in event and it is the communication of the heart of the covenant. The "dabar" is creative and efficacious and brings about what he expresses:

For just as from the heavens the rain and snow come down and do not return there till they have watered the earth making it fertile and fruitful, giving seed to him who sows and bread to him who eats, so shall my word be that which goes forth from my mouth. It shall not return to me void but shall do my will achieving the end for which I sent it. (Is 55:10-11)

If creativity is the foundation of the power of the Word of God this does not lessen its value of communication. The Word of God is intelligible in its creativity with the place of the hearing of that word found in the covenant. In the Old Testament the Word of God is expressed in communication in the covenantal form through the law and through the prophets. The law reveals the attitude of conformity to the bond which unites God and man; the prophetic word signifies the revelatory function of history and event.

The Word as creative also reveals its speaker. In his Word, God approaches man and thus shows himself to man. At the same time the Word of God is expressed humanly, in law and prophet and neither can adequately carry the Word of God. For the Old Testament God is present in his Word but God is not his Word. There is a communication between God and man but the difference between God and man is not dissolved. In this perspective God is and is not his Word. He was sometimes present and other times absent in the Word of the covenant. This idea is presented in the psalms as well as in the prophets. The people cry out to God in lamentation and discover a hidden God (Ps 22:1-22). Jeremiah feels abandoned by God in his anguish of rejection (Lam 3). History showed the people of Israel over and over again that any manifestation of God is not complete; he is a hidden God even as he is revealed.

One of the signs of the nearness of God to Israel was his law. The people had the greatest respect for the law. God was happiest when his law was observed and so often the law was seen as a mediator between God and man. Something similar could be said for wisdom in the Old Testament. It too was close to God and at times almost appears personified (Pr 8:22-26; Wis 25:8-10). We can say today that this tendency to personify was under the influence of Hellenism and Greek philosophy but also can be related to the tendency of Israel to join God to his outward expressions even if there was a general reluctance to identify the two.

The Word of God in the Old Testament offers a similar tendency. Isaiah 55:10, as quoted, seems to give the Word a separate identity as does Wisdom 18:14-16:

For when peaceful stillness compassed everything and the night in its swift course was half spent your all-powerful word from heaven's royal throne bounded, a fierce warrior into the doomed land bringing the sharp sword of your inexorable decree.

In both texts there is a function of judgment associated with the coming of the Word of God; it is so efficacious that one can present it as a personified will. A similar idea is found in Philo who adopted the Stoic conception of the "Logos" (Word) as universal reason and considered the Word as a personal mediator. This also could be the root for the later identification between the risen Lord as Word of God and executor of judgment as found in Revelation 19:11-16. With such a background it is not hard to understand the use of the Word of God in the gospel of John.

The Johannine community in Asia Minor must have been influenced by the speculations on Greek philosophy that surrounded them. The community also had the richness of Jewish tradition. It is useless to claim a totally Hellenistic influence of the gospel of John and the choice of "Logos" as a title of Jesus just as it is useless to disclaim any influence. There is no reason to assume a ghetto mentality in regard to intellectual activity for the Johannine community. In all likelihood the community was composed of Jews and Gentiles and there was at least a double influence behind the meaning of "Logos": the Old Testament tradition and the tendency to speculate on a divine "Logos" who designed the world and offered intelligibility. Since this Word had the privilege of transcendence there was a universal validity to the Word. When John relates "Logos" to Jesus as an historical individual and in relationship to his function of revealing the Father, he offers Jesus as the fulfillment of all that the Old Testament had hoped for in the Word of God as well as the divine and transcendent "Logos" who gives intelligibility to the universe. John joins the office of revealer to the being of the revealer. He was the Word of God in a biblical and philosophical sense.

Jesus, The Word in Revelation

Jesus, as we have seen, appeared as a prophet, or as The Prophet. He proclaimed the kingdom and announced the end times. We have also seen that the kingdom could not be separated from him who announced the kingdom. If we had only the Synoptics we might never come to the identification of Jesus as the Word of God even if there is foundation for such an identification in their writings. The prologue of John is a meditation in poetry on the mystery of Jesus as risen Lord. As risen Lord the author viewed all that had happened previously and recognized that the mission to reveal the Father and to announce the kingdom in himself was based on the very being of Jesus; he was the Word of God made flesh. Another back step into the Old Testament should throw further light on the enfleshment of the Word of God in Jesus.

God always revealed himself in his word in the Bible whether his word be considered as event or as spoken word. There could be no communication between God and man without some human exchange with the divine. God comes to man in the word he addresses to man. Creation itself in the Bible was a communication of the Word of God. Genesis has all of creation depend on the Word of God: "Then God said . . ." Romans also lays blame on the pagans who should have recognized God in created things: "Since the creation of the world, invisible realities, God's eternal power and divinity, have become visible, recognized through the things he has made" (Rom 1:20). Also in the Old Testament the covenant is the Word of God as well as the events that surround the history of the covenantal people. Since the Jewish people believed strongly in the presence of their God in their history, it was an expected consequence for the Word of God to be joined to the thought of God and will of God: "For just as from the heavens . . . , so shall my word be that goes forth from my mouth. It shall not return to me void but shall do my will achieving the end for which I sent it" (Is 55:10-11). The Word of God, as we have seen, is always communicated humanly; it is the Word of God in the words of men. The prophetic communication of God is not a revelation of God independent of the relation with man that God has sustained in history. God is present in his Word but the words of man are never adequate to express the Word of God. God is far beyond all words. The Old Testament reveals the Word of God but in a limited fashion.

More must be said in the case of Jesus. Certainly God reveals himself in the words of Jesus but Jesus is more than his words. Now, the mediation of salvation is not through another prophetic revelation. The prophet speaks the Word of God which in reality is not himself even if the spoken word belongs properly to the prophet. But the word of Jesus is his word; he is the Word of the Father. Such a notion leads us to rethink all the ideas on revelation. If Jesus is the incarnation of the Word of God then he is the final word, the eschatological, never to be repeated Word. In him the past as well as the future will take its meaning. God has communicated his Word in creation and in the covenant and in the history of the covenantal people. Now he communicates himself through the enfleshment of his Word in Jesus the Christ. Jesus as the Word of God is the full human revelation of God; he is the image of God and the first born of all creatures (Col 1:15). All history flows toward him for in him the prophetic word and the creative wisdom as well as the Hellenistic understanding of word finds completion. The historical Jesus is the consummation of revelation because the thought of God which is refracted in the prism of creation and history is none other than Jesus. The "Logos" has finished everything; he is the beginning of the utterances of God and the completion and he alone explains the Word of God as already present in creation and history. Up to the time of Jesus the Word of God was present from a distance, not giving itself in the most total fashion. With Jesus, although there is never the fullness of God expressed humanly, there is an entrance into human history without distance: "the Word became flesh and pitched his tent among us" (John 1:14). Revelation is not separable from Jesus for it is not only in his words that he speaks of God, but is himself the Word of God made flesh.

Word: Functional or Personal Title

When we attribute the title "Word of God" or "Logos" to the historical Jesus we join the revelation of God to the expression of that revelation in a complete fashion. Jesus reveals the Father because he is the Word of the Father. The title "Word" has been interpreted in Christian history as a personal title, especially since the Council of Chalcedon in 451 recognized in that name the second member of the Trinity. "Logos" was not considered as a functional title but a personal title. Today there is opposition to this viewpoint from Christian tradition.

Some oppose anything more than a functional Christology as an interpellation of metaphysics into the Bible; [3] others fear that an identification between Jesus as the Word of God in a personal sense, is a subtle denial of his humanity; still others state that a divine "Logos" is without meaning since human language is not capable of expressing the transcendent. The conclusion of such critics is that Jesus as the Word of God is a functional title, emphasizing the revelational purpose of his coming and his life and death. Any other interpretation would throw into shadow the very purpose of the incarnation: the actual index of revelation is the humanity of Jesus and not some metaphysics. To try to identify Jesus with some pre-existent being whether one wishes it or not places in peril the whole economy of salvation and the incarnation itself. Van Buren as well as Bultmann believes that historical theology and in particular the councils do not take seriously the humanity of Jesus for they deny it by affirming the transcendence of the "Logos" while they try to confess the true humanity.

Much of what these theologians are saying is true. In the past there has been a tendency to read too much into scripture and find philosophical solutions and explanations which are not present. Also, in the history of theology there has been a tendency to overlook the humanity of Jesus and concentrate on the divinity which is still witnessed in the mentality of our Christian devotions and prayers. The following chapter will try to present some contemporary ideas on the relationship between the humanity and divinity of Jesus so that we can truly say that the divinity is expressed in the humanity. For the present, it does not seem that an insurmountable opposition must exist between person and function.

God is known only in the measure that he communicates himself to us; he is God for us and this is how we know him. In this communication in Jesus there cannot be a false separation between what he communicated and himself. Recall that the Bible sees Jesus as the Lord of God. As such it is more concerned with him and the totality of Jesus than with his words. If there is to be a communication of God in a personal way, as seen in Jesus, that communication which is functional, cannot be separated from the individual who is doing the communicating. If we do not hold to a unity between person and revelation then Jesus becomes just another prophet which the New Testament will not accept. Jesus is not just someone who announces the kingdom of God as a communion between God and man, he is himself the communion between God and man because as man he is the enfleshment of the Word of God. The Word of God is in some sense identified with God and in some sense identified with Jesus. This still leaves us with the question of the personal identity of Jesus and of his ability to accomplish in himself, in a singular fashion, the union of eternal Word of God and an historical humanity. A more complete response to this question will follow in a later chapter. From scripture we know that in the gospel of John there is a movement from function to being. Jesus is the revealer and is such because he is the Word of God.

In a conclusion to Jesus as the Word of God incarnate we can say that the gospels and in particular the gospel of John orients us toward a sense which holds that the title "Word" or "Logos" is not merely functional. This use, however, introduces a certain obscurity into the meaning of "Logos" of God separated from Jesus of Nazareth and a certain question to the identity of Jesus of Nazareth. We can say that the transcendence of the Word in John does not place the humanity of Jesus in peril but on the contrary it restores the humanity of Jesus as the definitive mediator of revelation in his singular historical humanity. This will become clearer in a study of the title: Son of the Father. Jesus is the Word of God and thus reveals the Father. This is the conclusion thus far of this chapter. What must be considered now is the revelation of man that Jesus offers.

The Word: Revelation of Man

A study of Jesus as the Word of God revealing the meaning of man properly belongs in a study of Christian anthropology. It should be considered here, however, because there is such a close relationship between Christology and Christian anthropology. The more we understand ourselves the more we can understand Christ and vice versa.

We have already seen that Jesus is the Word of God. The New Testament also attests that he is the Image of God: "He is the image of the Invisible God" (Col 1:15). If we were to analyze this statement as well as Hebrews 1:13: "Christ reflects the glory of God and bears the very stamp of his nature," the relationship between Jesus and the Father is not superficial nor particular and limited but profound and total. The Word is the symbol [4] of the Father and Jesus is the Word incarnate, the image of God. We come to know the Father in the manifestation of his image, Jesus. All of this we have seen and is related to the divine sphere. The question arises: "What does Jesus as the image of God mean for the image of God in man?"

If Jesus is the image of God in the world then it follows that human nature is not something indifferent to the incarnation.[5] The possibility of man is based on the more fundamental possibility of a humanity expressing in its historical individuality the Word of God. Human nature is thus created as the "grammatica" which is required for the pronouncement of the Word of God in time. Human existence is so structured that in itself it is able to express in an hypostatic union the image of God in creation. It should also be noted here that we are talking about a human nature and not just the soul or spirit of man.

When we apply this to ourselves then we can add that any human nature in its unity of person is the presupposition required for the incarnation of the Word. Man as a person is the image of God because in an historical individual the Word of God became flesh. To talk about the image of God in man is something absolute inasmuch as any created humanity could have been the expression of the Word of God in human flesh; and it is something relative since the actualization of this potential of humanity depended on a free expression of God in time. If God would will to express himself humanly, then there existed this possibility in the nature of man.

A second conclusion for man from the belief that Jesus is the Word of God incarnate is that our own destiny is expressed in him. The goal of the process of human life is our assimilation to Christ in glory; "He is the image of the invisible god, the first born of all creatures" (Col 1:15). "God has willed to make known to them the glory beyond price which this mystery brings to the Gentiles—the mystery of Christ in you, your hope in glory" (Col 1:27). The image of God in us is perfected eschatologically when we bear in our total reality the image of Jesus as the second Adam, the second head of the human race. What he is now as risen Lord is our sure hope that we too shall rise in glory and manifest the image of God in our own persons. Jesus reveals to us what the possibility is that lies before us.

While we rejoice in the term of our life in the assimilation to the glorious Christ, we must not prescind from the process that leads to that final term. When Paul remarks in 2 Cor 5:21: "He who did not know sin became sin for us so that in him we might become the righteousness of God," he insinuates that we are not able to be possessed by the mystery of the glorious Christ without reference to the mystery of his death. We know that he took the form of a servant to give his life for many (Mk 10:45). If this is the way to glorification for Jesus, then the same must be true for his followers. Jesus as the Word of God in flesh reveals much about the meaning of human life, in particular the destiny of man which is God but a destiny that cannot be reached without following the way of the crucified Jesus. He reveals God and reveals man.

This chapter thus far has been rather heavy in theology and can stand the criticism that it is divorced from actual life. It is necessary to understand that Jesus can reveal God and reveal man before some more concrete application can be made. Thus far we have been most concerned with biblical Christology; it is time to demonstrate how biblical Christology can work for the individual believer. If the understanding of Jesus helps the understanding of man, and if the Bible is an expression of an understanding of Jesus, then a careful presentation of Jesus in the gospels should reveal much about the meaning of man. Two examples will suffice.

The gospels of Matthew and Luke begin the public ministry of Jesus with a narrative about his temptations. What is presented here is more than just a recap of the temptations of Israel in the desert and more than messianic temptations. The temptations are part of life and in his response to the temptations Jesus reveals something about life.

The first temptation:

He ate nothing in those days and when they were ended he was hungry. And the devil said to him, "If you are the Son of God, command this stone to become bread." Jesus answered him, "Man shall not live by bread alone." (Lk 4:3-4)

This temptation is part of every person's experience. It is temptation to seek pleasure alone. Eat, drink and be merry because tomorrow you will die. The pleasure principle is part of society exemplified in seeking only the best of everything. People have tried the pleasure principle and discovered an emptiness. The reaction of Jesus is that he will forego immediate gratifications of pleasure because he believes there is more to life than pleasure seeking; there is a different purpose that he has in mind. Man lives by more than bread; there is more to life than just seeking pleasure.

The second temptation:

Then the devil took him up higher and showed him all the kingdoms of the world in a single instant. He said to him, "I will
give you all this power and the glory of these kingdoms; the
power has been given to me and I give it to whomever I wish.
Prostrate yourself in homage before me, and it shall be yours."
In reply, Jesus said to him, "Scripture has it, 'You shall do
homage to the Lord your God; him alone shall you serve.'"
(Lk 4:5-8)

The second temptation is the temptation to power or social
position or status or prestige. Everyone faces this; all like to be
recognized, well-thought-of, able to influence people and affect
other lives. The response of Jesus is that you first worship God.
The real power or position in life comes from the worship and
service of God and all else is an illusion. We can go further in
analysis here and ask how we worship God. The gospels will
respond that we worship and serve God when we serve our
neighbor: "As often as you did it for one of my least brothers
you did it for me" (Mt 25:40). True prestige and power and
status are found in serving God and serving others.

The third temptation:

Then the devil led him to Jerusalem, set him on the parapet of
the temple, and said to him, "If you are the Son of God, throw
yourself down from here, for scripture has it, 'He will bid his
angels watch over you'; and again, 'With their hands they will
support you, that you may never stumble on a stone.'" Jesus
said to him in reply, "It also says, 'You shall not put the Lord
your God to the test.'" (Lk 4:9-12)

This is perhaps the most subtle of all the temptations; it is the
temptation to avoid personal responsibility. Jesus would never
succumb to this. If he were to cast himself down he would accept the consequences of his actions and would not tempt God.
Anyone who casts himself down from the pinnacle of the
temple will die when he strikes the bottom. No one may tempt
God, nor can anyone avoid responsibility. The same is true for
all. It is a simple thing to read the temptations of Jesus but they
are more than just his experience. Jesus is telling us much about

life and ourselves in these temptations. He reveals something of the mystery of man as he reveals the mystery of God.

A second example of Jesus revealing something of the meaning of human life is found in the narrative of Martha and Mary.

On their journey Jesus entered a village where a woman named Martha welcomed him to her home. She had a sister named Mary, who seated herself at the Lord's feet and listened to his words. Martha, who was busy with all the details of hospitality, came to him and said, "Lord, are you not concerned that my sister has left me to do the household tasks all alone? Tell her to help me." The Lord in reply said to her: "Martha, Martha, you are anxious and upset about many things; one thing only is required. Mary has chosen the better portion and she shall not be deprived of it." (Lk 10:38-42)

The ordinary reaction to this episode is to side with Martha. If we look closely it is a better thing to side with Mary. Jesus seems to ask Martha to take a close look at herself instead of looking askance at her sister. There is such a thing as being too conscious and needful of work and taking care of things, that you miss the most important thing in life. Mary came in and sat at the Lord's feet. She was far more aware of the need for personal relationships in life and less aware of the need for household tasks. This does not mean that caring for the household is not good; it does mean that everyone should be careful to place first things first.

It is an easy thing to become so work-oriented that we miss the people with whom we live and work. We can become overwhelmed by events and things to do and places to go. There has to be more to life than this. Everyone must be part Mary and part Martha; no one should be a Martha all the time. Life will be very dull if the prime concerns are achievement and accomplishing tasks. To miss people is a tragedy which once missed will never return.

These episodes are rather mundane in the gospels but tell about life. If Jesus is the Word of God then we can believe that he has shown us the Father and has allowed us to enter into a communion with the Father. As Word of God he also recalls what it means to be human and alive. He reveals in himself the mystery of man and this is closely related to the mystery of God. Theology which does not enter into life situations is not authentic; if the Word of God is alive today it must have something to say to people who are alive today. Believers confess that Jesus is the Word of God and in this confession acknowledge that he reveals God and reveals man.

NOTES

[1] Cf. J. Starcky, "Logos," *Dictionnaire de la Bible Supplement,* (Paris: Letouzey, 1957), col 481. J. L. McKenzie, *Dictionary of the Bible,* (Milwaukee: Bruce Publishing Co., 1965), p. 938-941.

[2] For a fuller presentation of the meaning of "Logos" in the fourth gospel see: R. Brown, *The Gospel According to John,* (Doubleday, 1966) Appendix II "The Word," pp. 519-524.

[3] Bultmann, Van Buren, Dewart and others look upon the metaphysical approach as the Hellenization of Christianity. Their own emphasis will be on a functional Christology which is concerned with what Jesus did and not with whom he was. For a good presentation of the various positions see: R. Fuller, *The Foundations of New Testament Christology,* (London: Lutterworth, 1965), p. 247ff.

[4] The use of the word "symbol" here has a technical meaning. This will be explained in the following chapter.

[5] Much of what follows is based on the thought of Karl Rahner. For a fuller presentation cf. "Man," *Sacramentum Mundi,* Vol. 3.

CHAPTER 8
JESUS, THE SON OF
THE FATHER

A sense of mystery permeates any approach to Jesus as the Son of God. Since there is no limit to our understanding, we must probe the meaning of Jesus always with a sense of wonder and awe. No age or person has the final word on the mystery of God and man, but each age can offer something in the search for a deeper penetration into the meaning of Jesus. It helps us to know what those from other times understood about Jesus; it also helps if we relate our appreciation of Jesus to our individual lives. It can never be just a game with words and philosophy. What matters is the personal understanding of the mystery that is Jesus the Christ.

More than fifteen hundred years ago the Christian church was in turmoil. Believers were confused in regard to the relationship of the human and the divine in Jesus and in the midst of that turmoil the Council of Chalcedon (451) confessed:

. . . one the same Christ, the Son, the Lord only begotten in two natures unconfused, unchangeable, undivided and inseparable. The difference of natures will never be abolished by their being united but rather the properties of each remain unimpaired both coming together in one person and substance, not parted or divided among two persons but in one and the same only begotten Son, the divine Word the Lord Jesus.

This profession of faith underlines the unconfused presence of two natures in Christ and affirms with equal force the personal unity. This unity is based on the eternal Son who became man with emphasis on the incarnation of the "Son." Chalcedon also teaches clearly that Jesus is truly divine, like the Father, and truly human, like us, "in all things but sin" (Heb 4:15). This affirmation by the council became the foundation for all subsequent theological interpretation so that believers have come to say without hesitation: "Jesus is one person with two natures." Today, this very doctrine is being reappraised. The school of Antioch with its emphasis on the humanity of Jesus claims more followers than the school of Alexandria with its emphasis on the divinity. Theologians and believers of all Christian churches are questioning the meaning of "one person in two natures," as well as the very meaning of divinity as applied to Jesus. No Christian theologian can feel free to deny the teaching of the church in her councils but many readily make a distinction between what the council wanted to express and the language in which they expressed their teaching. A hint of this attitude is found in the decree on Ecumenism in the Vatican Council II:

If at various times and circumstances there have been deficiencies in moral conduct of church discipline or even in the way the church teaching has been formulated not to be greatly distinguished from the deposit of faith itself—these should be set right at the opportune moment and in the proper way.[1]

In the many attempts to come to appreciate the mystery that is Jesus many elements and ideas and notions have come from a particular cultural milieu. In different philosophical and cultural ambits various aspects of the mystery will be emphasized. Just as there is a *sitz im leben* for scripture so there is a life situation for the councils. If we can know more about the circumstances surrounding the conciliar proclamation we come to a better understanding of what was said. Once they have established the meaning of the official statement of the church, theologians can try to express this meaning in different words.

This is a great desire today: to adapt the teaching on Jesus to the new cultural milieu that has been forming for the past few centuries. To try to repeat the answers of a past age to the man of today is to betray the responsibility of the theologian who, like the scribe of Matthew is forever taking from the storeroom something that is ever new as well as old (Mt. 13:52).

This chapter will try to relate some ideas from contemporary theology to the data of scripture as well as to be a brief presentation of a renewed doctrine of intrinsic symbolism. What the contemporary theologians are saying merits consideration by a questioning generation. All is done in an effort to understand and profess more profoundly faith in the mystery of Jesus the Christ. A good beginning is an examination of some problems posed by the more traditional understanding of Christology.

Traditional Christology

Some people get very upset when theologians begin to examine the divinity/humanity of Jesus. It is easy to pretend that the traditional presentation of Christology is very clear and precise and offers to modern man an understanding of Jesus that is meaningful to all men of all ages. But what is the true picture? Does the traditional formula of one person in two natures really make the mystery of Jesus more intelligible, or does it add to the confusion? Is there more darkness after than before? Has the classical theology really explained even in a rudimentary fashion how Christ could have two natures in one person with two faculties of willing and knowing? Does the theory from scholasticism on the union of natures in the one person show how only the Son is incarnate and not the Father and the Spirit? The most important question that must be asked is whether the philosophical positions which underlie these explanations are valid today in the light of the meaning of person and nature that is current in philosophy and in common parlance. There is no easy way to relate humanity to divinity. If contemporary thinkers are trying another way, then their thinking must be explored.

Jesus as Son in Scripture

Much of traditional theology on Christ does not speak to man today. The image of an eternal "Logos" descending and living a human life and still remaining in the divine sphere does not inspire many people to belief. The image of Jesus of Nazareth does inspire people. The gospels offer Jesus as someone who has a history, clearly related to a specific time and place: first century Palestine; he is someone who has sentiments; who can be discouraged when his disciples fail to understand him; who could be depressed when his disciples wish to sit on his right and left hand; who has concern for the poor and the outcasts and could be deeply touched by the death of a widow's son. Jesus is someone with needs and someone who can correspond to the needs of others by his own appreciation of their problems and his effort to alleviate them. The Synoptics present Jesus as someone with a warm human personality, someone real with whom it is easy to identify.

He is also presented as a Jew and relates himself to the Jewish tradition. The God of the law, the Torah, is his God and Father. Jesus, in his life situation, reveals himself and gathers individuals around him with whom he shares his understanding of God and life. He shows people something of their own lives by offering his appreciation of life. He is very real and very human in the Synoptic gospels.

The gospel of John offers a different picture of Jesus. No longer do we find the very human dimension; rather, he is presented as the divine man who knows all and controls all. In the gospel of John, Jesus has no temptations, he is not baptized by John for repentance, he knows Nathanael under the fig tree (1:48); he suffers no agony in the garden and has a clear picture of all that will happen to him: "Jesus—fully aware that he had come from God, and was going to God. . . ." (Jn 13:3). Jesus asks no questions and speaks as the risen Lord throughout his public ministry. This picture is quite different from the Synoptics. There is one area of agreement, between John and the Synoptic gospels, however, which has great significance for an understanding of the divinity and humanity of Jesus. Jesus calls himself the "Son."

Throughout the gospels Jesus refers to "my God" and "your God," "my Father" and "your Father." He never says "Our Father." [2] Jesus is careful to distinguish his relationship to God from anyone else's relationship to God.

"I for my part assign to you the dominion my Father has assigned to me." (Lk 22:29)

"I send down upon you the promise of my Father. Remain here in the city until you are clothed with power from on high." (Lk 24:49)

"If you, with all your sins, know how to give your children what is good, how much more will your heavenly Father give good things to anyone who asks him!" (Mt 7:11)

"The unbelievers are always running after these things. Your heavenly Father knows all that you need." (Mt 6:32)

"When you stand to pray, forgive anyone against whom you have a grievance so that your heavenly Father may in turn forgive you your faults." (Mk 11:25)

The first two references are to "my Father"; the others to "your Father." Jesus describes his relationship to God in terms of a filial relationship. God is always Father and Jesus is always Son.

The gospel of Mark has fewer passages which treat of the Father/Son relationship than the other gospels. Even here there is a clear presentation of this relationship in three passages.

The parable of the wicked vinedressers traces the history of salvation. Jesus separates himself from all other envoys and places himself as Son in the proper role. Mark closes the parable with the statement: "They wanted to arrest him at this, yet they had reason to fear the crowd. They knew well enough that he meant the parable for them." (Mk 12:12).

In the thirteenth chapter of Mark Jesus situates the Son above the angels: "As to the exact day or hour, no one knows it, neither the angels in heaven nor even the Son, but only the Father." (Mk 13:32). Jesus wanted to show how secret is the day of judgment and in support he declares that even those who are closest in intimacy with God do not know this information: the angels that pertain to his court and the Son. The disciples would understand that such a secret could not then be communicated to them. They are below the dignity of the angels and certainly do not have the intimacy of the Son.

Finally, Mark has Jesus pray "Abba" (Father) in the garden (Mk 14:36). He prays as someone who has an intimacy with God and can use a most familiar expression, "Abba."

The gospel of Matthew frequently speaks of the relationship between Jesus and God as a filial relationship, and distinguishes this relationship from the ordinary person's attitude.[3] The same can be said for the gospel of Luke.[4]

The title "Son" as such does not prove an exceptional relationship that Jesus might enjoy. The Bible calls Israel "Son of God" (Ex 4:22) and the king of Israel is designated as Son (Ps 89:27) as well as the angels (Ps 2:7). In each instance there is a proximity and intimacy with a corresponding dependence on God. The cause of such a designation could be the demands of the social order (angels and king) or just the result of predilection (Israel and the just man).

In regard to Jesus, the title means more than merely a just man. There is a new level of intimacy reached with Jesus:

"Everything has been given over to me by my Father. No one knows the Son but the Father, and no one knows the Father but the Son—and anyone to whom the Son wishes to reveal him." (Mt 11:27)

Matthew presents Jesus as the revelation of the Father because he is Son. The Son alone knows the Father intimately and he alone can disclose the Father to others.

Luke offers a parallel passage:

"Everything has been given over to me by my Father. No one knows the Son except the Father and no one knows the Father except the Son—and anyone to whom the Son wishes to reveal him." (Lk 10:22)

The source of intimacy reaches a new pitch in the gospel of John: "The Father and I are one." (Jn 10:30).

"If I do not perform my Father's works, put no faith in me. But if I do perform them, even though you put no faith in me, put faith in these works, so as to realize what it means that the Father is in me and I in him." (Jn 10:37-38)

There is a fundamental union between Jesus and God who is his Father and this is the basis of his personal understanding of himself, and the reason he could be the revelation of God as Father to others.

From scripture we can conclude that Jesus sees himself as Son, in a relationship to God similar to other men but far superior since the level of intimacy reached with him is a union between God and himself. Scripture is also careful to point out that Jesus is not God; he is the "Son."

Theological Reflection

It belongs to Jesus to exist in a divine way; however, this is verified in him not in an absolute sense, but as Son. There exists divinity which is described as filiation and divinity that corresponds—paternity. Jesus reveals God as Son. This explains that his attitude toward God is circumscribed by the attitude of a Son. Jesus the man is not God, he is the Son. We can also say that "Son" is not an attribute but the subject. The title "God" is the attribute or perhaps it is better to say that "divine" is the attribute given to "Son." [5] The scriptures are clear to point out that Jesus does not take the position of another God. This must be the foundation for any conclusions as to the relationship between humanity and divinity in Jesus. Before coming to the relationship it is necessary to speak about humanity and its fundamental unity.

The Meaning of Humanity

The scriptural concept of man as a unity wandered into unfamiliar territory over the course of centuries. For many years a subtle and not so subtle dualism infected philosophy and theology. To speak of body and soul is not the best description of man; to speak of man even when disembodied is to labor under a false understanding of man. The traditional understanding of man created in the image of God as reflected in the *spiritual* aspect of man was the result of a similar tendency to downgrade the bodily aspect. The history of Christian theology and western philosophy demonstrates a similar failure to appreciate the mutual relationship of the spiritual, psychical and material in man. Today we are conscious of the unity of man which means that man is an incarnate spirit, or body-subject; or an individual who maintains within a unity, the diversity of spiritual, psychological and material dimensions.

The personality of Jesus must also be re-evaluated as a total man. If the whole history of Christology has been the search for the maintenance of the unity in Christ together with the presence of the human and divine and today there is an emphasis on human unity, then perhaps the classical doctrine of two natures and one person can be re-examined.

Theologians are making attempts to rethink the problems presented here. Each theologian will maintain the data of faith that Jesus was truly man and truly divine in every way, but they will explain the dynamic unity according to principles of contemporary philosophy. The thesis that will underline this chapter is that Jesus is God in man; or Jesus is the Son of God by being a man in a unique way.

The Data of Scripture

We have already seen that the New Testament presents Jesus as an unusual man, as one who has a unique relationship to God which he describes as "Son." This is fundamental to the meaning of the mystery that is Jesus the Christ. We have also seen that Jesus affirms himself and understands himself in relationship to others and in particular to God as his Father. He is God's Son in all that he is; this defines his personality. Moreover, this is not the same meaning of "son" as applied to all children of God. There is an intimacy and union established between God and Jesus which is presented in each of the gospels which separates him from all other claims to intimacy. He is a man, attested by scripture and tradition, but a man in a most usual way.

We usually explain the uniqueness of Jesus by resorting to the spiritual or divine dimension of his life. He is the Word of God incarnate and alone reveals the Father. But as we have already seen, this divine aspect of Jesus cannot be separated from the man Jesus. It was as man that he revealed the Father, it was human words he used and he died a human death. We cannot overlook the divine dimension of Jesus but this is relevant to the history of salvation and to us only as the divine elevates and perfects the human nature of Jesus without in any way destroying it. However we explain the divinity and humanity in Jesus it is a new mode of being man and a different way of being divine.[6] The mystery of Jesus takes its reality from the human side because now the human is the visible manifestation of the divine in human history.

In the history of theology John Damascene and Thomas Aquinas spoke of the instrumentality of the humanity of Jesus. They spoke of the human nature of Jesus as a created reality, the means by which the divine nature of the Word of God manifested itself. Such teaching offers a foundation for further speculation especially in view of contemporary anthropology. Instead of saying, however, that Jesus is man in whom the presence of God appears, or that he is the instrument of the divinity in his humanity, it would be more accurate to state that the man Jesus is the presence of the Word of God in the world. Jesus is the Son of God in his humanity and thus the divinity must be perceptible in the humanity itself: "Philip, he who sees me sees the Father" (Jn 14:9). The mystery of Jesus does not lie beyond Jesus but is found in his being a man;

the human form is the revelation of the divine. We must not speak of the man Jesus in whom there is realized the presence of God distinct from Jesus. The instrumentality of the human nature of Jesus is not enough to explain how we come to know the divinity for Jesus is the presence of the Word of God. God has truly become other in Jesus. At this point it would be beneficial to recall the doctrine of intrinsic symbolism as found in the history of theology but made more known today in the writings of Karl Rahner.[7]

Intrinsic Symbolism

Rahner begins his presentation of the doctrine of symbolism with the notion that all being is itself symbolic, that is, all being is constituted by a fundamental unity which then discloses itself in multiplicity which disclosure is then viewed as the perfection of the original unity. In this process there is what Rahner calls the *selbstvollzug* or self-actuation in which there is the flowing out and a return to self.

All things strive to return to themselves, want to come to themselves, to take possession of themselves, because the "having being" which they desire comes to be in the measure in which they take possession of themselves. All activities, from the sheerly material to the innermost life of the Blessed Trinity, are but modulations of this one metaphysical theme, of the one meaning of being: self-possession, subjectivity. "Self-possession," however, is itself realized to a double phase: a flowing outwards, an exposition of its own essence from its own cause—an *emanatio,* a withdrawing into itself of this essence, which has expressed itself in terms of its specific cause—which has, as it were, revealed itself.[8]

Rahner sees this notion of self-possession or actualization as constituting the being as it exists so that the moments of realization in multiplicity are rooted in a dynamic unity which is prior to the resolution into multiplicity.

What takes place in the constitution of being is the movement to become perfected by being present to itself through the positing of what might be called the "inner other" which makes possible the expression of the primary unity and the return of this unity in the resolve into multiplicity. This process of a fundamental unity resolving itself into multiplicity and perfecting itself in this flowing and return is the ontological reason why being is of necessity symbolic. The multiplicity is the "symbol" which contains the fundamental unity and which at the same time is the perfection of the unity. An example taken from man will verify this position.

The basic unity of an individual resolves itself into a multiplicity which involves people and things and events and situations. This outgoing of man perfects the individual and without the multiplicity of a human life there is never the development of the unity that is man. Man becomes himself only in and through others; man is the symbol of himself. The multiplicity is the resolution of the individual and expresses the individual and at the same time perfects the unity. On a more experiential level the reality that is man is expressed bodily. Man knows and loves and lives and acts and reacts, but these activities must be concretized and are manifested in words and gestures and signs. The love that perfects a man will never achieve its result unless that love is expressed in relation to the multiplicity of people and events. There can never be knowledge unless it is received bodily and expressed bodily. The fundamental symbol is the human body which contains the reality that is expressed (the person) and brings about a perfection of the unity that is the person. At the same time the symbol is never the total or adequate expression of the reality expressed. Man is always more than the bodily expression even if it is only through the bodily expression that the person is known and perfected. The symbol contains the reality it expresses but never in a total or adequate manner. How does the doctrine of intrinsic symbolism apply to Jesus the Christ?

Jesus, the Christ: Symbol of God's Word

We can speak of the "Logos" as the expression of the

Father, or the symbol of the Father inasmuch as the primordial unity that is God resolves itself into multiplicity in his Word and Spirit. We can also say that this multiplicity in God—Father, Son and Spirit—is the resolution and perfection of the divine unity. The "Logos" expresses the unity of God as Father and is the symbol of this unity even if the "Logos" is not the same as the fundamental unity, God as Father. The reality, divinity, is expressed in the "Logos" and is truly divine but the "Logos" is not the same as the Father. If we carry this position further we can speak of a certain necessity for the incarnation since the Father through the "Logos" achieves self-actualization in the other that is Jesus of Nazareth.[9] In the incarnation human nature is constituted as the other in whom the "Logos" resolves itself into multiplicity by manifesting the perfection of the fundamental unity. Jesus is the symbol of the "Logos" as the "Logos" is the symbol of the Father. The Word of God has become incarnate in a human nature which human nature is the expression in multiplicity of the inner-Word of God. Jesus is the symbol of the "Logos," containing the reality that is being expressed and perfecting the reality but, as is true for any symbolic activity, the symbol is never totally equated with the reality that is being expressed.

If we accept Rahner's notion that man is constituted to be the articulation of the Word of God and that Jesus of Nazareth realizes the most radical destiny of man, then Jesus who is the symbol of the "Logos" is also the full realization of what it means to be man. In Jesus humanity reached a destiny it had always possessed in orientation.[10]

The most evident consequence of this application of symbolism to the problem of humanity and divinity in Jesus is that the human is the manifestation of the divine, however inadequate. It is impossible to predicate and delineate what is human from what is divine. We are not dealing with two separate realities; we are dealing with one reality which is the human expression of the divine. We may try to delineate the human from the divine in Christ but this is impossible. The life and death of Christ, limited in space and time, are the concrete manifestations of the transcendence of God. The words, actions and attitudes, and all that transpired in his life, are the translation into concrete reality of the meaning of a gracious Father in regard to his creation. The Word of God became flesh so that all that pertains to and articulates and expresses Jesus as a man is at the same time the proclamation of God. Whatever the words and actions and attitudes of Jesus tell us about the man, they tell us about God because this man is the "symbol" of the Word of God, the enfleshment of God. The loving attitude of Jesus toward the woman taken in adultery (Jn. 8:1-11), the forgiveness manifested on the cross (Lk 23:34), his warm relationship with Martha and Mary and Lazarus (Lk 10) are more than just a good human approach to life; they are the tangible expressions of God's approach to human life. They tell us about human life and how we are to live that life, but more precisely they tell us about the attitude of God toward man and toward life.

The symbol according to Rahner is the expression of the reality, but cannot be considered as equivalent to the reality. What is being expressed is truly present in the expression but the expression is not equivalent to the reality behind it. This also must be applied to Jesus. Just as the "Logos" is the expression of the Father, but not the same as the Father, so Jesus is the symbol of the "Logos" but cannot be identified completely with the "Logos." The mystery of God is not exhausted in Jesus; there can never be a total expression of God on the level of creation; the finite can never contain adequately the infinite. Jesus is the final and eschatological manifestation of God on the created plane and in him we can truly know something of God even as the mystery of God remains inexhaustible intelligibility.

When a comparison is made between this approach and traditional Christology there are changes in perspective and terminology. A different philosophical approach will change the manner in which the basic belief of Christianity is presented. The profession of faith, Jesus is truly God and truly man, remains the same, but the formulation of this profession of faith changes.

Jesus does not possess human nature minus human personality. There is no question of one nature and one nature
making one person. If the unlimited God wishes to appear to
us he must do so in the limited fashion of the human. God
is truly with us in this human fashion in Jesus so the Word
of God himself is personally man. But we need not talk
about the union of natures in one ontological person. Person
and nature mean something different to us today than they
meant in the fifth century. Rather, we can talk about a truly
human subjectivity in Jesus in which the Word of God manifests himself. Whatever is present in the man Jesus is, by that
fact, the presence of the divine. He is man but in a most
unusual and significant way since this man is the presence of
God. It might even be more accurate to speak of Jesus as
God in man rather than God and man.[11]

This teaching may appear somewhat novel. It is supported
however, by the earliest Judaic-Christian teaching on man as
created in the image and likeness of God (Gen. 1:27; 1 Cor
11:7), and Christ as the image of God (Col 1:15, Heb 1:3).
If Jesus is the symbol of the "Logos" then this is based on
the possibility of the incarnation which in turn depends on the
belief that man is created to the image of God and capable
of enunciating the Word of God. Man was created so that a
man could be the Word of God in human form. This is the
reality that is Jesus of Nazareth. Moreover, the Bible is clear
that the total man is the image of God and not just his
spiritual nature.

The contemporary interest in the Jesus of history and the
Christ of faith also supports such a view. It is generally accepted today that it is impossible to separate the two. In the
historical Jesus there was the revelation of the transcendence
of God, so the Christ of faith assures us. It was the historical
Jesus that taught us to serve God by serving man. If we are
to interpret Jesus today his divinity must not be seen apart
from his humanity and human life. God was not present in
intervals in the life of Jesus, he was present in the totality
that makes up the historical Jesus of Nazareth.

A conclusion to this section should tie together the data of scripture with the findings of contemporary theology. From the New Testament we know that Jesus describes himself as "Son"; moreover, the New Testament does not call Jesus, God. Yet there is an intimacy and union between Jesus and the Father which cannot be predicated of any other man. Where there is Jesus there is the presence of God. Scripture is also careful to concentrate on the revelation of God that took place in the full life and death of Jesus. The divine is not separated from the human in the gospels. The further conclusions in the history of theology must be viewed as human attempts to come to a better realization of the mystery of the divine and human in Jesus. To speak of two natures and one person may well be a fitting conclusion of the gospels' account of Jesus for people steeped in a particular philosophy; it may not be a fitting description today.

To speak of Jesus as the symbol of the "Logos" emphasizes the humanity of Jesus which is appealing today. This in no way prescinds from the divinity. A full understanding of symbolism preserves the transcendence of God while safe-guarding belief in the true divinity of Jesus. The human Jesus was surely human and was more than just human; the humanity of Jesus was the expression of the divine by which we come to know and to love the divine. In Jesus, God creatively posited a human subjectivity as his own so that when Jesus spoke of himself as "I" it was the human subjectivity involved and not a subjectivity distinct from his humanity. That subjectivity is also the expression of the divine subjectivity. Jesus is the human way of being God; human nature is not one and the divine nature two. God encompasses and includes all that there is in being man and in being this particular man.

The Trinity in God

One question which immediately arises in such a discussion is the place of the Trinity and in particular the pre-existence of the Word of God. Certainly it can be said that if Jesus is the symbol of the "Logos," the spiritual or divine dimension of Jesus pre-existed. The question is whether faith requires the pre-existence of "Son" apart from the incarnation? To respond to this question we must recall that we know nothing of God except what he has revealed. We would never know of the "Son" of God without the incarnation of that Son. It might be better to limit our thinking on the inner nature of God by what is revealed to us. We believe in God who is Father, Son and Spirit, but have come to know Father, Son and Spirit only in the history of salvation. To come to some definite conclusions about the inner nature of God prescinding from the revelation of God in history and in Jesus is to go beyond the limits that have been imposed on us.

There is one further response that should be made. Christian tradition holds firmly that the Trinity in the history of salvation is the expression of the Trinity in itself. If this were not so, then we would know nothing of God in himself, only God for us as known in revelation. There must be in God the structure of possibility that would correspond to Father, Son and Spirit in the history of salvation, but whether this can or should be expressed in terms of three persons and one nature seems to be beyond our understanding. There must be a correspondence between God as we know him and God as he is, otherwise we would be hopelessly deluded, but to name this correspondence clearly and definitively is beyond the ability of man and his thought. The mystery of God is still a mystery even as he has revealed to us something of this mystery.

God is Father in scripture and Jesus is his Son; the Spirit is present in the church. God is Father because he has chosen to reveal himself to us; he is Son because we have witnessed this in an historical man, Jesus of Nazareth; God is Spirit because he continues to be with us in the community of believers. The Trinity is real to us not in terms of first, second and third person, but as Father, Son and Spirit present to us in the Christian experience. To try to delineate more precisely the inner nature of God by prescinding from his revelation as Father, Son and Spirit can only cause confusion. In such a theory as presented here, the Trinity remains unaffected; the pre-existence of Son and Spirit and Father apart from the revelation of God, is problematic.

The approach taken here makes the relationship between Jesus and the believer closer than usually presented in the past. This is not surprising. If man is created with the possibility of the incarnation, then every human nature has the possibility of being the expression of the divine even if historically this occurred only once. Every man can reveal God, can speak his word because one man historically was the incarnation of that Word.

The following conclusions are in order:

1. Jesus does not reveal God in an absolute sense; but as "Father" because he is "Son."

2. Jesus is the symbol of the "Logos"; the reality of the Word of God is expressed in the humanity of Jesus.

3. All that is human in Jesus expresses and is the presence of the divine.

4. The relationship of the Trinity in the history of salvation and the inner trinity is not changed by such teaching.

5. Symbolic theology as applied to Christology prescinds from the philosophical position of two natures and one person.

6. The Trinity as Father, Son and Spirit should not be considered apart from the history of salvation.

7. Even with all the theology at our disposal, we face a mystery in which God is present to us in Jesus who is human, "like us in all things but sin" (Heb 4:15).

The ideas presented here will cause reactions. If the council fathers call theologians to rethink the faith of Christianity by examining the formulation of that faith, then the re-thinking must be done. The faith remains the same: belief in the true divinity and humanity of Jesus. To try to express this belief in forms that are more understandable today, we must have the blessing of God. The result will always be imperfect and never complete. Such is always the human lot.[12]

NOTES

[1] The Documents of Vatican II, Ed. Walter Abbott (New York: America Press, 1966). "Decree on Ecumenism" #6. A similar notion was expressed by Pope John XXIII in his opening address to the council. "The deposit of faith is one thing; the way that it is presented is another. For the truths preserved in our sacred doctrine can retain the same substance and meaning under different forms of expression." AAS, Vol. 54 (1962), p. 792.

[2] Matthew does make reference to "Our" Father in his presentation of the Lord's prayer. (Mt 6:9). This is recognized by exegetes as coming from a liturgical setting. The Lukan formula (Lk 11:2) is considered as the original wording.

[3] Cf. Mt 5:16, 45, 48; 6:1, 4, 6, 18, 26; 7:11, 21; 10:20, 29; 11:26ff; 15:13; 16:17, 27; 18:11, 14.

[4] Cf. Luke 6:36; 9:26; 10:21, 22; 11:2, 13; 12:30, 32; 22:29, 42; 23:49; 24:49.

[5] Cf. Karl Rahner, "Theos in the New Testament," Theological Investigations, Vol. 1, (Baltimore: Helicon, 1961), pp. 79-148.

[6] Rahner presents his understanding of God "becoming" in Spiritual Exercises, (New York: Herder and Herder, 1965), pp. 104-113. Cf. Also: Theological Investigations, Vol. 1, (Baltimore: Helicon, 1961), pp. 149-200.

[7] Cf. K. Rahner, "The Theology of the Symbol," Theological Investigations, Vol. 4, (Baltimore, Helicon, 1966), pp. 221-252.

[8] K. Rahner, Hearers of the Word (New York: Herder and Herder, 1969), p. 49.

[9] Such modified "necessity" for the incarnation would not destroy the freedom of God. It can be considered as a conclusion from a very traditional axiom in theology: the first in intention is the last in execution. Eternally God willed the incarnation; all of creation would then be directed toward this incarnation.

[10] Cf. Karl Rahner, Theological Investigations, Vol. 4, pp. 105-110.

11 The expression "God in Man" is found in certain Dutch theologians, e.g., P. Schoonenberg, *The Christ*, (New York: Herder and Herder, 1971).

12 It would be beyond the purpose of this book to document the ideas presented in this chapter. For a fuller presentation by contemporary theologians please see the bibliography cited following these chapters.

CHAPTER 9
JESUS, THE PRIEST

Jesus the servant, savior and Son of God is situated within human history for a purpose. As in all of history, people are different with his coming. There is no adequate name which can sum up the full meaning of Jesus and his saving work but there is one title that can gather together much of what has been said and unite the person and work of Jesus: he is a priest; he is the only priest; he is the eternal priest; he is priest for us now as he was priest in his life and death.

Whether Judaism at the time of Christ had identified the messiah to come with a high priest is uncertain, but there are certain signs that there was some relationship. Speculations on the obscure figure of Melchisdech and on Psalm 110 oriented Judaism toward the notion of the high priest as one of unique dignity exercising this power in the messianic times. The Qumram community had both traditions: messiah as king and priest in their expectation. There is no identification between messiah and high priest to come but there is some preparation for the idea.

When we examine the gospels, however, it seems quite clear that Jesus avoided the title priest. He was involved in difficulties with the Sadducees as well as the Pharisees and his criticism of the established hierarchy is evident. This does not mean that the gospels were unconscious of priestly aspects of the life and death of Jesus. The theme of sacrificial death is seen in John 10: 17-18 as well as Mark 10:45. The substitution of a new temple is in the same vein (Mk 14:58; Jn 2:19; 7:37-39).

It should also be remembered that in ancient Judaism the priest exercised more than a title role: he announced the Word of God and proclaimed the law (Dt 31:9; Hos 4:6).[1] Jesus surely fulfilled this priestly function (Mt 5:21-48; Mk 1:22).

These are not the clearest references to Jesus as priest in the gospels but they will offer some foundation for a later predication of the title to Jesus. When we consider the situation of Judaism at the time of Jesus it is not surprising that the gospels do not record the title for Jesus. Priesthood at that time was ritual and cultural, tied in with the political system. If Jesus assumed the title priest, it could only confuse the meaning of his priesthood. After the paschal death of Christ the authors of the New Testament could risk the danger of misunderstanding by applying the title to Jesus but this was done only at a later date and with much caution. Jesus was evidently not interested in identifying with the official priesthood of Israel; he does, however, seem to fulfill the meaning of the priesthood of the people in the Old Testament. Once again a return to the Old Testament offers clarification.

Priesthood in Israel

The book of Deuteronomy in the Old Testament offers the foundation of the priesthood of all believers in Israel.[2] God has chosen Israel for a specific task in relationship to the other nations. She alone is to know the true God and her first responsibility was to reveal him to others:

. . . but you, who clung to the Lord, your God, are all alive today. Therefore, I teach you the statutes and decrees as the Lord, my God, has commanded me, that you may observe them in the land you are entering to occupy. Observe them carefully, for thus will you give evidence of your wisdom and intelligence to the nations, who will hear all of these statues and say, "This great nation is truly a wise and intelligent people." (Dt 4:6-8)

. . . he will then raise you high in praise and renown and glory above all other nations he has made, and you will be a people sacred to the Lord, your God, as he promised. (Dt 26:19)

The second task of Israel as a priestly people was to offer the true worship to God and not engage in any false worship:

You shall not plant a sacred pole of any kind of wood beside the altar of the Lord, your God, which you will build; nor shall you erect a sacred pillar, such as the Lord, your God, detests. (Dt 16:21)

What God wanted was the worship of fidelity, the worship of the hearts of people, of far greater consequence than all holocausts:

For you are not pleased with sacrifices; should I offer a holocaust, you would not accept it. My sacrifice, O God, is a contrite spirit; a heart contrite and humbled, O God, you will not spurn. (Ps: 51:18-19)

Israel was called to fulfill this role as a kingdom of priests:

You shall be to me a kingdom of priests, a holy nation. This is what you must tell the Israelites. (Ex 19:6)

The final responsibility of Israel in the covenant with God as his holy nation was to care for the poor. As Israel was once abandoned and in need of liberation and justice in Egypt, so she must always remember her condition of old and care for the needs of others: "The needy will never be lacking in the land; that is why I command you to open your hand to your poor and needy kinsman in your country" (Dt 15:11). The Lord promised to bless Israel if she takes care of those in need (Dt 15:1-11). This threefold responsibility is given to all the people who are priests if they fulfill what is expected of them by God.

In the Old Testament there is also a hierarchical priesthood present.[3] In Israel the origins of this office are shrouded in darkness. In the patriarchal era the people worshiped at their local shrines and evidently the head of the household functioned as priest. Through a careful analysis of the Pentateuch it is clear that the priesthood as an office developed over a period of years even though the editors of the Pentateuch situated it in the desert fully developed. This hierarchical priesthood emphasizes the sanctification of the priest by his role which consisted of giving oracles, the leading of ritual and the teaching of the law. After the exile the priests took on more kingly roles with a gradual confusion of power. With the birth of the synagogue, during and after the exile, the role of the Word of God took on greater importance. By the time of Jesus the role of the priest was more tied in with politics, power and prestige and it is not unusual for Jesus to disassociate himself from the hierarchical priesthood. If there is a relationship in the Old Testament between Jesus the priest and the priesthood, that relationship is found more in regard to the priesthood of all believers than the hierarchical priesthood.

Priesthood of Jesus, the Christ

Jesus the Christ is the perfect and only priest. He alone glorified God; he alone sanctified people. The gospels do not present Jesus as priest in the usual sense of the word. The gospel of John, however, presents in chapter 17 what can be considered as the foundation of the priesthood of Jesus. In this chapter the evangelist presents Jesus as accomplishing his mission on earth. He has glorified God his Father by revealing his name to men:

"I have given you glory on earth by finishing the work you gave me to do. Do you now, Father, give me glory at your side, a glory I had with you before the world began. I have made your name known to those you gave me out of the world. These men you gave me were yours; they have kept your word." (Jn 17: 4-6)

He has made himself the holy one of God so that others may share in that same holiness:

"I consecrate myself for their sakes now, that they may be consecrated in truth." (Jn 17:19)

Jesus gives glory to the Father through the sanctification of people. This is the fundamental element of the meaning of his priesthood. Whenever the Bible refers to the glory of God it is frequently understood as the manifestation of his power. This is then joined in later writings to the experience of his presence. His glory is made evident when it becomes known who he is; when he is recognized as a merciful and faithful God. Throughout the Old Testament, God is present to his people and always he shows them his covenantal virtues of mercy and fidelity. The Exodus itself is seen as the great sign of these qualities of God. When these qualities of God are accepted and when the people try to reflect similar qualities then the glory of God is revealed.

When this idea is brought over into the New Testament Jesus alone is the glory of God (1 Cor 11:7; Heb 1:3). The fourth gospel joins in the prologue the glory of God with the qualities of mercy and fidelity: ". . . and we have seen his glory, the glory of an only Son coming from the Father, filled with endearing love" (Jn 1:14). Jesus gives glory to the Father by revealing the name of God, by showing his qualities; Jesus has sanctified himself to show this glory and sanctifies others to grant them the same possibility of showing the glory of God by reflecting in their lives the qualities of God: mercy and fidelity. Some further thoughts from Hebrews will enable us to see more clearly the implications of the priesthood of Jesus in the New Testament.

The Epistle to the Hebrews [4]

It is generally accepted today that the author of Hebrews labors to present the priesthood of Jesus in relationship to Jewish priesthood and superior to this priesthood. The general framework of the epistle must be seen first.

The epistle is divided into five sections moving from the analysis of the position of Jesus in regard to God and men to an exhortation for the Christian people to live a life in accord with their sharing in the life of their high priest.

The first section (1—2) situates Jesus in relation to God and in the context of the angels. The author carefully presents his basic image of Jesus as Son of God (distinct from the angels) and brother to man (like us as one of our race). This is his starting point for all future developments.

The second section (3—4) emphasizes the reality of our high priest. We have such a one who obtains peace for us. The author presents the mercy of God in Jesus as well as emphasizing the solidarity of Jesus with people. He is named by God but is one taken from among men.

The third section (5—10) presents the more complete theme of Jesus as priest using the vocabulary characteristic of the institution of Israelitic priesthood: the offering of sacrifice, the purification of the people by blood, the entrance into the holy of holy, and in all of this the superiority of the priesthood of Christ over the ancient priesthood.

The fourth section (11:1; 12:13) presents ideas on faith as seen as the characteristic response to the reality of the priesthood that is ours in Christ. The author relates this faith today to the faith in the Old Testament and its chief example. He then adds the presence of faith in Christ as a change in mode of the faith as seen in the Old Testament.

The final section (12:14—13:18) is an exhortation to the Christian people in which the authentic Christian life joins together charity and sanctity into a single reality.

The author moves from situating Christ to the presentation of his priesthood, to the final exhortation to live a Christian life based on the same. In this perspective we can study the rather important verses in chapter 2.

. . . therefore he had to become like his brothers in every way, that he might be a merciful and faithful high priest before God on their behalf, to expiate the sins of the people. Since he was himself tested through what he suffered, he is able to help those who are tempted. (Heb 2:17-18)

Exegesis of Hebrews 2:17-18

Jesus as the high priest is in sharp contrast with the office in Israel. Christ has not obtained social status nor monetary remuneration nor political power nor even elevation among the people by his priesthood. Christ is high priest through the renunciation of privilege. Nor did he extol himself above the people: "He was assimilated to his brothers" even to the extreme point of death. He became priest by offering himself in his ministry and his death by which glory was given to his father.

In this passage two qualities stand out: mercy and fidelity. These are interpersonal adjectives pertaining to relationships which express the mediation which Christ exercises between God and man.

Merciful

He has human compassion toward us as our priest. To have this there must have been a prior experience of sadness and tribulation. Christ had to sustain human suffering to have this relationship of mercy. This involved active service and a consoling ministry to those in need. This is seen in the actual life of Jesus as recorded in the Synoptics. He was the kind and compassionate Lord who is seen in the gospel of Luke, chapter 15. He is the merciful prophet who fulfills all of the expectancy of the Old Testament in Matthew. He is the Son of man unto death who brings the experience of mercy to those who call on him in faith in Mark. He is one with his followers and united in them in loving them to the end in John.

Faithful

Faithfulness is essentially applied to God who keeps the faith; the covenant faith is what characterizes the attitude of God toward man. No matter what man may choose to do, the Word of God remains faithful. God will never abandon his people. He is the one who offers the firm foundation to those who trust in him.

This idea is applied to Christ as priest: he is worthy of faith; he is enthroned before God and is proclaimed Son and is perfected in the stability of his fidelity. He is worthy of our trust as priest and through him we can be certain that we have sure access to the Father.

Sirach 6:6-16 observes that real fidelity is seen in tribulation. Because he bore upon himself all our tribulations and took on an ignominious death, his fidelity became clearly apparent. This further emphasizes the relationship of his fidelity to us. He is faithful in the midst of tribulations and in the presence of tribulations he not only does not abandon his love and obedience to his Father, but he also remains faithful to his commitment to us.

The conjunction of these two adjectives relates the priesthood of Christ to the covenantal virtues of God. In him all converge; there is mercy and divine fidelity toward man and there is human mercy and fidelity toward God. The covenantal virtues are manifested coming to man and are shared in by man in the return response to God. Moreover, these same virtues are manifested outward from Christ to include all of mankind. He is the perfect mediator and perfect priest and his functions are aptly described in these two adjectives.

The author further continues with his presentation of purpose: the expiation of sins. He is the faithful and merciful high priest who cleanses man from his sins; he makes man holy through the exercise of his function. The Son of the Father and brother of man exercises the covenantal virtues and thus expiates for sins and makes man holy.

John 17

The priesthood of Jesus as seen in Hebrews concurs with the meaning of the gospel of John. The Father is glorified when the Son uses the power bestowed on him to give life to men. This Jesus has done in revealing the name of God to men. He has shown them that God is Father and is merciful and faithful. Now the final moment of glorification has come for Jesus and his followers. God's glory, his name, and his divine qualities will be revealed in the Passover meal and in the offering of Jesus in death and finally will be culminated by the great sign of the glorification of Jesus: the resurrection.

In this chapter there is a clear reference to the holiness of God: "Holy Father" (17:11), "Righteous Father" (17:25) and the holiness of Jesus: "I consecrate myself" (17:19). What must follow is the holiness, the nearness to God of those who have come to hear and to believe in the name of God: "That they may be consecrated in truth" (17:19). The believers are made holy in "truth," in Jesus, and are sent to make the name of God known in this world which will manifest the glory of God. Jesus himself is the "truth" of God which makes men holy. This truth as known and preached makes God present in the world as merciful and faithful and causes people to react to the nearness of God.

Everything that is present in these chapters can be related to the priesthood of all believers in Israel. Those who believe in Jesus are the sign to others that God is near and offers salvation; they make his name known to the nations as the saving and present God offering himself in the life and death of Jesus. The followers of Jesus offer the true worship; they offer their holy lives as the sacrifice to God and render glory to God and finally they care for those who are in need. All of this Jesus had done as priest and now his followers will continue his ministry. As Jesus manifested the qualities of God and sanctified himself and others he was a priest who fulfilled all of the responsibility of priesthood of believers in the Old Testament; now when believers manifest these same qualities they fulfill their priestly function and render glory to God with Jesus.

The result of the activity of Jesus as priest is the communion that is established between God and man, and man and man. He prays that "they may be one, as we are one— I living in them, you living in me—that their unity may be complete" (Jn 17:22-23). He has accomplished his task, and now there is a unity established between God and man. The priesthood of Jesus in John and Hebrews is the glorification of God through the sanctification of people. He accomplishes this task by making himself "holy," by manifesting the covenantal virtues of mercy and fidelity. He is risen Lord and prophet and savior and Word and Son of the Father, and he is priest joining God to man and man to God, but expiating for sins (Heb 2:17), and consecrating man (Jn 17:19).

Priesthood of Believers

There is one priest, Jesus Christ. There are many who share in this priesthood; all those who believe that Jesus is the Christ. The New Testament is not concerned with the special priesthood of the sacrament of orders as much as it is concerned with the priesthood of all believers. Throughout the gospel of John and the epistle to the Hebrews references are made to what the believers must be. Good works are needed in which the qualities of God are seen. Peace is most essential if men are to be united with God: "Strive for peace with all men, and for that holiness without which no one can see the Lord" (Heb 12:14). John offers a similar prayer: " 'Peace' is my farewell to you, my peace is my gift to you; I do not give it to you as the world gives peace. Do not be distressed or fearful" (14:27).

Brotherly love is to characterize the community of believers who are reflecting the qualities of the priesthood of Jesus: "Love your fellow Christians always" (Heb 13:1); "I give you a new commandment: Love one another. Such as my love has been for you, so must your love be for each other" (Jn 13:34).

Finally, the sacrifice of praise, the spiritual sacrifice of a good life lived for God and for others will sum up what the priest of Jesus Christ must do: "Through him let us continually offer God a sacrifice of praise, that is, the fruit of lips which acknowledge his name" (Heb 13:15). We profess his name and make his name known to all who will come to listen and in this render glory to our Father who has called us to union with him through the gift of his Son. Jesus is our priest, who has shared our lot and showed us the qualities of God so that we could be his holy people, bringing others to learn the name of God and believe that all men can be united with God who is kind and gracious and loving and ever faithful to his creation. When we speak of the priesthood of all believers we speak of the priesthood of Christ shared in by all, calling each Christian to exercise the priestly role that Jesus has begun, and which he continues through the life of his followers. Jesus is our priest.

You, however, are "a chosen race, a royal priesthood, a holy nation," a people he claims for his own to proclaim the glorious works of the One who called you from darkness into his marvelous light. Once you were no people, but now you are God's people; once there was no mercy for you, but now you have found mercy. (1 Pet 2:9-10)

NOTES

[1] Cf. Roland DeVaux, *Ancient Israel* (New York: McGraw-Hill Publishing Co., 1961), pp. 345ff.

[2] Cf. Gerhard Von Rad, *Studies in Deuteronomy* (London: SCM Press, 1953). Much of what follows on the common priesthood are conclusions from this interesting study by Von Rad.

[3] Cf. DeVaux, pp. 372-405.

[4] Cf. Albert Vanhoye, *Exegesis Epistulae Ad Hebraeos, Cap. I-II* (Rome: Pontifical Biblical Institute, 1968). The exegesis presented here is largely dependent on this exposition.

CONCLUSION
JESUS, THE CHRIST
AND CHRISTIANS

The question posed in the eighth chapter of Mark: "Who do you say that I am?" will be with believers as long as they live. Most Christians today have grown up with Christ. Perhaps because we have grown up with him we have never really accepted him, or we have taken him for granted. It is always a problem to accept Jesus; and after we have accepted him it is a greater problem to follow him. There are more demands made upon those who try to follow than the initial acceptance. It is not the most difficult thing to say "I believe in Jesus" but to take the next step: "Because I believe in him, I will follow him," can be a problem. Yet, unless it is a personal response it is not a human response and there is something missing in the Christian life.

These pages have tried to unfold the first part of faith, the acceptance. People have to be open to be evangelized. As the gospels unveil Jesus there must be an opening to be able to hear the Word of God. To hear the Word of God and respond is to move from acceptance to following, but first there must be listening. As we have seen there are many responses to Jesus. These pages have centered on some approaches. Jesus is a free man who believed strongly in his mission and would not accept compromise in that mission. He was free because he placed his relationship to God as primary. He was free because he knew that life is broader than laws or regulations, that behind religion there must be faith. He assures all that the worship of God presupposes the love of the neighbor. He was free because he did not see a need to repay people in kind. His relationship with people was more than just reacting and counterreacting. This is the beginning of the response to Jesus.

Jesus is also risen Lord. He has entered into a final, complete and definitive relationship to God and to us. He has already reached that point which all hope to reach. He is the first born of many brethren. He is alive and present to us and he offers us hope for the future.

Jesus is savior and redeemer. He will redeem time and space and all of creation. He has saved people and the world from the conquest of evil and has assured us that because of his death there can never be a total victory for evil and sin and death. Mankind, and his world, has a good future which is offered to everyone. As savior he offers the opportunity to experience the peace and harmony and goodness in our lives that is promised in a fuller sense for the end times. Salvation is real for the present even as it leads us into the future.

Jesus was the final prophet who pointed out the religious dimension of everyday life. He lived an ordinary life in many respects, yet in that ordinary life he could reveal the presence of the divine and help us to appreciate the religious dimension that is part of life.

Jesus is the Son of the Father. In his humanity he revealed something of the divine. In him the divine took on human flesh, he was the human face of God. Not just in what he said, not only in his death, but everything about Jesus of Nazareth was the Word of God incarnate. He showed what it means to be human and what it means to be divine. We can look at him and believe that the eternal God has entered our history and with him life will never again be the same. He was the Word of God who taught us the meaning of life.

Servant and priest are closely related. He became one with us to serve and to sanctify us. He glorified the Father and by the sanctification that he offers us we too can glorify the Father.

Such are the titles. There are others which could be used in making a response to Jesus. These were chosen in order to respond to the needs of believers today. The acceptance of Jesus today should include belief in Jesus as the free risen Lord, who is savior, redeemer, prophet, servant, Word of God, Son of the Father and priest. This is the acceptance of Jesus. What comes next is the following of Jesus.

This acceptance of Jesus is offered to us in the Bible. The following of Christ is the making of the Christian. If we believe that in Jesus, the Christ, human nature has reached that point toward which it has always been directed, then what is said of Jesus must be applied in some sense to all men.

To follow Jesus is to be free. It is difficult to accept the freedom of Jesus; it is easier not to be free. Often it is more comfortable to limit the horizons of life to a narrow, gloomy and pessimistic viewpoint. It is hard to be free enough to see more. No one finds it a complete joy to have integrity and principle, to be able to say "yes" and as unequivocably say "no." How demanding it is to be free enough not to treat people as we are treated, to refrain from repaying in kind. There is a royal freedom that is present in Jesus which has always been a source of embarrassment for his followers. This uneasiness has been present in the leaders of the Christian church as well as in the ordinary people in his church. Only a truly free person can be a follower of Christ. This is a freedom that is not given once and for all, but grows and becomes as we grow. The follower of Jesus sees the love of God and the love of neighbor as primary in life and views all else in this shadow. Such is a great freedom.

If Jesus is risen Lord, where is he today? He is present wherever his followers are. He is present in this world when his followers are living and influencing that world for good. Now the risen Lord shows the mercy and fidelity of God in the lives of his followers even when people do not deserve mercy and fail to appreciate what is offered. His followers are faithful in the midst of infidelity. A follower of the risen Lord makes Jesus present everywhere in visible form.

To be servant is not to be on the top or the bottom. To be

a servant is to be with. A servant shares what he has and receives from others what they have to offer: this is the meaning of servant in the New Testament. Jesus is with us and gives of himself and because he is part of us receives from us what we offer. The follower of Jesus has much to reconsider in the servant theme. No one can make a contribution unless he is part of the group. This is true for family life, religious life, business, political or social life. The servant who follows Jesus gives because he is united with those to whom he is sent to serve and receives as well as offers.

Each title has something to say to the believer today. We are all called to be prophets, to speak the Word of God to others. We are all priests who contribute to each other's holiness. The world should be a better place because of the followers of Jesus who make this a holier place. Such is the Christian, a truly beautiful picture. Whether it has ever been realized is problematic. For some people at specific times it has been realized, but never in a total sense. Whether there will ever be a fully Christian community is a hope expressed in the Acts of the Apostles:

Those who believed shared all things in common; they would sell their property and goods, dividing everything on the basis of each one's need. They went to the temple area together every day, while in their own homes they broke bread. With exultant and sincere hearts they took their meals in common, praising God and winning the approval of all the people. Day by day the Lord added to their number those who were being saved. (Acts 2:44-47)

They believed and shared what they had in common. They tried to follow Jesus Christ and made their personal response to him. Each had what was needed in a community of spiritual and material goods. If there was ever, or ever will be, a truly Christian community the Acts tell us that it depends upon sharing what one has: faith, love, hope, and all that is present in one's life.

The community went to the temple daily. They prayed together. Prayer is essential for the Christian life. People must learn to pray together, to express their need for God and a willingness to accept the support and encouragement he offers. This must be done together. They broke bread in their homes. They celebrated the Eucharist. They came together and joined their faith in the offering of the Lord's Supper.

They were a joyous people who partook of their food with glad and generous hearts. They were not given over to pessimism and gloom. They saw the goodness in life in spite of apparent troubles and sorrows. They had favor with people; they were on good terms with others. The Lord added to their number every day. If there ever was a Christian community of believers that community is aptly described in the Acts of the Apostles.

If there is ever to be a Christian community today, the same characteristics must be present. We make individual responses to Jesus and join with others in an effort to follow him. To this there is no ending. The more we come to believe in Jesus Christ the more we are called to follow him. We make a personal and individual response to the question: "Who do you say that I am?" Once this is made, we live with other people who have made a similar response and together we follow Jesus who is always the Lord and Christ. We are evangelized.

BIBLIOGRAPHY

General Works

Barrett, C. K., *Jesus and the Gospel Tradition,* Philadelphia: Fortress Press, 1968.

Bornkamm, Günther, *Jesus of Nazareth,* New York: Harper & Row, 1960.

Bouesse, H., and J. J. Latour, *Problemes Actuels de Christologie,* Paris: Desclee, 1964.

Congar, Yves, *Jesus Christ,* New York: Herder & Herder, 1966.

DeRosa, Peter, *God Our Savior,* Milwaukee: Bruce Publishing Company, 1967.

Dibelius, Martin, *Jesus,* Philadelphia: Westminster Press, 1959.

Duquoc, C., *Christologie,* Paris: Editions du Cerf, 1968.

Felder, Hilarin, *Jesus of Nazareth,* Milwaukee: Bruce Publishing Company, 1953.

Fichtner, Joseph, *Christ—the Center of Life,* Milwaukee: Bruce Publishing Company, 1968.

Grasso, Domenico, *The Problem of Christ,* Staten Island: Alba House, 1969.

Grenville, C., "The History of Jesus and Contemporary Christology," *Louvain Studies,* Vol. 1, 1967, pp. 269-283.

Grillmeier, Aloys, *Christ in Christian Tradition,* New York: Sheed and Ward, 1965.

Guillet, Jacques, *Jesus Christ Yesterday and Today,* Chicago: Franciscan Herald Press, 1965.

Guitton, Jean, *Jesus: The Eternal Dilemma,* Staten Island: Alba House, 1968.

Hofmans, Flor, *Jesus: Who Is He?* New York: Newman Press, 1966.

Hunter, Archibald, *The Work and Words of Jesus,* Philadelphia: Westminster Press, 1950.

McIntyre, John, *The Shape of Christology,* London: S.C.M. Press, Ltd. 1966.

Maloney, George, S.J., *The Cosmic Christ,* New York: Sheed and Ward, 1968.

May, William F., *Christ in Contemporary Thought,* Dayton: Pflaum, 1970.

Padovano, Anthony, *Who Is Christ?* Notre Dame, Indiana: Ave Maria Press, 1967.

Pannenberg, Wolfhart, *Jesus—God and Man,* Philadelphia: Westminster Press, 1968.

Pittinger, Norman, *Christology Reconsidered,* London: S.C.M. Press, Ltd., 1970.

Roey, A., "Contemporary Christological Questions," *Louvain Studies,* Vol. 2, 1968, pp. 158-169.

Rohde, Joachim, *Rediscovering the Teaching of the Evangelists,* Philadelphia: Westminster Press, 1969.

Sabourin, Leopold, *The Names and Titles of Jesus,* New York: MacMillan Co., 1967.

Schillebeeckx, E., *Christ the Sacrament of the Encounter with God,* New York: Sheed and Ward, 1963.

Schoonenberg, Piet, *The Christ,* New York: Herder and Herder, 1971.

Schweizer, Eduard, *Jesus,* Richmond: John Knox, 1971.

Biblical Christology

Alonso-Schokel, Luis, "Is Exegesis Necessary?" *Concilium,* Vol. 10, Number 7 (1971), pp. 30-38.

Brandon, S.G., *Jesus and the Zealots,* New York: Scribners, 1967.

Braun, Herbert, "The Meaning of New Testament Christology," *Journal for Theology and the Church,* Vol. 5, 1968, pp. 93-104.

Bousirvin, Joseph, S.J., *Theology of the New Testament*, Maryland: Newman Press, 1963.

Conzelmann, H., *An Outline of the Theology of the New Testament*, New York: Harper and Row, 1969.

Cullmann, Oscar, *The Christology of the New Testament*, Philadelphia: Westminster Press, 1959.

Cullmann, Oscar, *Jesus and the Revolutionaries*, New York: Harper, 1970.

Cullmann, Oscar, *The New Testament—An Introduction for the General Reader*, Philadelphia: Westminster Press, 1968.

Fuller, R. H., *Foundations of New Testament Christology*, New York: Scribners, 1965.

Jeremias, Joachim, *The Central Message of the New Testament*, New York: Scribners, 1965.

Käsemann, Ernst, *Essays in New Testament Themes*, London: S.C.M. Press, 1964.

Käsemann, Ernst, *Jesus Means Freedom*, Philadelphia: Fortress Press, 1969.

Kromer, Werner, *Christ, Lord, Son of God*, Naperville: Allenson, Inc., 1966.

Lynch, William E., C.M., *Jesus in the Synoptic Gospels*, Milwaukee: Bruce Publishing Company, 1967.

O'Grady, John F., "The Attitudes of Jesus," *The Bible Today*, November 1970, pp. 86-92.

Saunders, Ernest, *Jesus in the Gospels*, New Jersey: Prentice Hall, Inc., 1967.

Rahner, Karl, "Exegesis and Biblical Theology," *Biblical vs. Dogmatic Theology*, Baltimore: Helicon, 1964, pp. 31-66.

Voss, Gerhard, "The Relationship between Exegesis and Dogmatic Theology," *Concilium*, Vol. 10, Number 7, 1971, pp. 20-29.

The Jesus of History and the Christ of Faith

Anderson, Charles, *Critical Quests for Jesus*, Grand Rapids: Eerdmans Publishing Co., 1969.

Bourke, Joseph, "The Historical Jesus and the Kerygmatic

Christ," *Concilium*, Vol. 1, Number 2, 1966, pp. 16-26.

Braaten, Carl, and Harrisville, Ray, Eds., *The Historical Jesus and the Kerygmatic Christ*, New York: Abingdon Press, 1964.

Briggs, R. C., *Interpreting the Gospels*, New York: Abingdon Press, 1969.

Bultmann, Rudolf, *Jesus and Mythology*, New York: Scribners, 1958.

Bultmann, Rudolf, *Jesus and the Word*, New York: Scribners, 1958.

Bultmann, Rudolf, *Kerygma and Myth*, London: SPCK Press, 1953.

Dulles, Avery, "Jesus of History and Christ of Faith," *Commonweal*, Vol. 87, 1967, pp. 225-232.

Fuchs, Ernst, *Studies of the Historical Jesus*, Naperville: Allenson, Inc., 1960.

Good, Edwin M., *The Theology of Rudolf Bultmann*, London: S.C.M. Press, 1966.

Henderson, Ian, *Rudolf Bultmann*, Richmond: John Knox Press, 1966.

Käsemann, Ernst, "The Problem of the Historical Jesus," *Essays on New Testament Themes*, London: S.C.M. Press, 1964.

Leon-Dufour, Xavier, *The Gospels and the Jesus of History*, New York: Desclée. 1969.

McArthur, Harvey, "From the Historical Jesus to Christology," *Interpretation*, Vol. 23, 1969, pp. 190-206.

McArthur, Harvey, *In Search of the Historical Jesus*, New York: Scribners, 1969.

Macquarrie, John, *An Existentialist Theology: A Comparison of Heidegger and Bultmann*, New York: Harper, 1965.

Mussner, Franz, *The Historical Jesus in the Gospel of St. John*, New York: Herder and Herder, 1967.

Robinson, James, *A New Quest of the Historical Jesus*, London: S.C.M. Press, 1959.

Rowlingson, D., "The Jesus of History and the Christ of Faith," *Christian Century*, Vol. 85, 1968, pp. 1619-22.

Schweitzer, Albert, *The Quest of the Historical Jesus*, New York: Macmillan Co., 1966.

Jesus, the Risen Lord

Benoit, Pierre, *The Passion and Resurrection of Jesus Christ,* New York: Herder and Herder, 1969.

Brändle, Max, "Did Jesus' Tomb Have to be Empty?" *Theology Digest,* Vol. 16, 1968, pp. 18-21.

Brändle, Max, "Early Christian Understanding of the Resurrection," *Theology Digest,* Vol. 16, 1968, pp. 14-17.

Brändle, Max, "Narratives of the Synoptics about the Tomb," *Theology Digest,* Vol. 16, 1968, pp. 22-26.

Brown, Raymond, "Resurrection and Biblical Criticism," *Commonweal,* November 1967, pp. 232-236.

Clark, Neville, *Significance of the Message of the Resurrection,* London: S.C.M. Press, 1967.

Drinkwater, F. H., "Recent English Writing on the Resurrection," *Continuum,* Vol. 5, 1967, pp. 441-45.

Drinkwater, F. H., "The Risen Body," *Continuum,* Vol. 5, 1968, pp. 60-63.

Durrwell, F. X., C.S.S.R., *The Resurrection,* New York: Sheed and Ward, 1960.

Frei, Hans W., "Theological Reflections on the Gospel Accounts of Jesus' Death and Resurrection," *The Christian Scholar,* Vol. 49, 1966, pp. 263-306.

Fuller, Reginald H., *The Formation of the Resurrection Narratives,* New York: Macmillan, 1971.

Gutwenger, Englebert, S.J., "The Narration of Jesus' Resurrection," *Theology Digest,* Vol. 16, 1968, pp. 8-13.

Hebblethwaite, Peter, S.J., "Theological Themes in the Lucan Post-Resurrection Narratives," *Clergy Review,* Vol. 50, 1965, pp. 360-69.

Holtz, Ferdinand, "The Soteriological Value of the Resurrection of Christ," *Theology Digest,* Vol. 3, 1955, pp. 101-106.

Hooke, S. H., *The Resurrection of Christ,* London: Dartmon, Longman and Todd, 1967.

Kremer, Jacob, "Paul: The Resurrection of Jesus, the Cause and Exemplar of our Resurrection," *Concilium,* Vol. 10, Number 6, 1970, pp. 78-91.

Lampe, G. W. H., and Mac Kinnon, D. M., *The Resurrection,* London: A. R. Mowbray Co., Ltd., 1966.

Lohfink, Gerhard, "The Resurrection of Jesus and Historical Criticism," *Theology Digest,* Vol. 17, 1969, pp. 110-114.

Marxsen, Willi, *The Resurrection of Jesus of Nazareth,* Philadelphia: Fortress Press, 1970.

Moule, C.D.F., *Significance of the Message of the Resurrection,* London: S.C.M. Press, 1968.

O'Collins, Gerald, "Aquinas and Christ's Resurrection," *Theological Studies,* Vol. 31, 1970, pp. 512-22.

O'Collins, Gerald, "Is the Resurrection an Historical Event?" *Heythrop Journal,* Vol. 8, 1967, pp. 381-87.

Schnackenburg, Rudolf, "On the Expression 'Jesus is Risen' (from the dead)," *Theology Digest,* Vol. 18, 1970, pp. 36-42.

Smith, Joseph J., "Resurrection Faith Today," *Theological Studies,* Vol. 30, 1969, pp. 393-419.

Stanley, David M., *Christ's Resurrection in Pauline Soteriology,* Rome: Pontifical Biblical Institute, 1961.

Van Iersel, Bas., "The Resurrection of Jesus—Information or Interpretation," *Concilium,* Vol. 10, Number 6, 1970, pp. 54-67.

Vawter, B., "Resurrection and Redemption," *Catholic Biblical Quarterly,* Vol. 15, 1953, pp. 11-23.

Wansbrough, Henry, "The Resurrection," *The Way,* Vol. 11, 1971, pp. 324-330; Vol. 12, 1972, pp. 58-67; pp. 142-148.

Jesus, the Prophet

Ashton, John, "Consciousness of Christ," *The Way,* Vol. 10, 1970, pp. 59-71, pp. 147-157.

Betz, Otto, *What Do We Know about Jesus?* Philadelphia: Westminster Press, 1968.

Brown, Raymond, "How Much Did Jesus Know?" *C.B.Q.,* Vol. 29, 1967, pp. 315-345.

Fuller, Reginald, *The Mission and Achievement of Jesus,* London: S.C.M. Press, 1954.

Gutwenger, Englebert, "Problem of Christ's Knowledge," *Concilium,* Vol. II, 1966, pp. 91-105.

Leeming, Bernard, "The Human Knowledge of Christ," *The Irish Theological Quarterly,* Vol. 19, 1952, pp. 234-253.

Leon-Dufour, Xavier, "Jesus' Testimony Concerning His Own Person," *Word and Mystery,* New York: Newman Press, 1968, pp. 185-199.

Milolaski, S. J., "Jesus Christ: Prophet, Priest, and King," *Christianity Today,* Vol. 6, 1961, pp. 26-27.

Nicolas, J., "Controversy About the Psychological Unity of the Christ," *Theology Digest,* Vol. 2, 1954, pp. 97-98.

O'Grady, John F., "Jesus as Prophet, The Question of His Knowledge," *Chicago Studies,* Vol. 9, 1970, pp. 243-250.

Perego, Angelo, "The Psychological Unity of Christ," *Theology Digest,* Vol. 6, 1958, pp. 58-62.

Rahner, Karl, *Theological Investigations,* Vol. 5, Baltimore: Helicon Press, 1966.

Singh, Surgit, *Christology and Personality,* Philadelphia: Westminster Press, 1961.

Jesus, the Servant

Altizer, Thomas J., *The Gospel of Christian Atheism,* London: Westminster Press, 1966.

Altizer, Thomas J., and Hamilton, William, *Radical Theology and The Death of God,* New York: Bobs-Merrill Co. Inc., 1966.

Cooper, John C., *The Roots of Radical Theology,* London: Westminster Press, 1967.

Dawe, D.G., "A Fresh Look at the Kenotic Christologies," *Scottish Journal of Theology,* 1967.

Marshall, I. Howard, "Son of God or Servant of Yahweh?" *New Testament Studies,* Vol. 15, 1969, pp. 326-336.

Martin, R. P., *Carmen Christi,* London: Cambridge Univ. Press, 1967.

O'Donnell, R. E., "The Servant Christology in the New Testament," *Dunwoodie Review,* Vol. 4, 1964, pp. 177-195.

Schoonenberg, Piet, "The Kenosis or Self-Emptying of Christ," *Concilium,* Vol. 1, Number 2, 1966, pp. 27-36.

Streiker, L. D., "The Christological Hymn in Philippians II," *Lutheran Quarterly,* Vol. 16, 1964, pp. 49-58.

Todt, H. E., *The Son of Man in the Synoptic Tradition,* Philadelphia: Westminster Press, 1965.

VanBuren, Paul, *The Secular Meaning of the Gospel,* New York: Macmillan, 1966.

Willaert, Benjamin, "Jesus as the 'Suffering Servant'," *Theology Digest,* Vol. 10, 1962, pp. 25-30.

Jesus, the Savior

Ahern, B., "Christ, Cosmos and Modern Colossians," *Bible Today,* Vol. 38, 1968, pp. 2631-4.

Brunner, Emil, *The Mediator,* Philadelphia: Westminster Press, 1966.

Daujat, Jean, *The Theology of Grace,* New York: Hawthorn Publishers, 1959.

Gonzalez-Ruiz, Jose-Maria, "Redemption and Resurrection," *Concilium* Vol. 1, Number 2, 1966, pp. 37-47.

Lyonnet, Stanislas, "St. Paul and a Mystical Redemption," *Theology Digest,* Vol. 8, 1960, pp. 83-88.

Lyonnet, Stanislas, "Scriptural Meaning of 'Expiation'," *Theology Digest,* Vol. 10, 1962, pp. 227-232.

Plastaras, James C., *Creation and Covenant,* Milwaukee: Bruce Publishing Company, 1968.

Rahner, Karl, "Man," *Sacramentum Mundi,* New York: Herder and Herder, 1970.

Rahner, Karl, *On the Theology of Death,* New York: Herder and Herder, 1961.

Rahner, Karl, "Salvation," *Sacramentum Mundi,* New York: Herder and Herder, 1970.

Schlitzer, Albert, *Redemptive Incarnation,* Notre Dame, Indiana: Univ. of Notre Dame Press, 1962.

Solle, Dorothee, *Christ the Representative,* London: S.C.M. Press, 1967.

Stanley, David M., "Christ as Savior in the Synoptic Gospels," *Catholic Biblical Quarterly,* Vol. 18, 1956, pp. 345-63.

Stanley, David M., "The Conception of Salvation in Primitive Christian Preaching," *Catholic Biblical Quarterly,* Vol. 18, 1956, pp. 231-54.

Suelzer, Alexa, *The Pentateuch,* New York: Herder and Herder, 1964.

The Way, Vol. 10, 1970. (The entire issue is devoted to the meaning of salvation.)

Willems, Boniface A., *The Reality of Redemption,* New York: Herder and Herder, 1970.

Jesus, the Word of God

Ebeling, Gerhard, *God and Word,* Philadelphia: Fortress Press, 1967.

Hodgson, Peter, "Heidegger, Revelation and the Word of God," *Journal of Religion,* Vol. 49, 1969, pp. 228-252.

Hodgson, Peter C., *Jesus—Word and Presence,* Philadelphia: Fortress Press, 1971.

Leslie, Robert, *Jesus and Logotherapy,* Nashville: Abingdon Press, 1965.

Ong, Walter, *The Presence of the Word: Some Prologomena for Cultural and Religious History,* New Haven: Yale Univ. Press, 1967.

Rahner, Karl, *Hearers of the Word,* New York: Herder and Herder, 1969.

von Balthasar, H. U., *Word and Revelation: Essays in Theology I,* New York: Herder and Herder, 1964.

Jesus, the Son of the Father

Baltazar, Eulalio, *God Within Process,* New York: Newman, 1970.

Barth, Karl, *The Humanity of Jesus,* Richmond: John Knox Press, 1960.

Beggiani, Seely, "A Case for Logocentric Theology," *Theological Studies,* Vol. 32, 1971, pp. 371-406.

Brown, Raymond, *Jesus, God and Man,* Milwaukee: Bruce Publishing Company, 1967.

Ceroke, C. P., "The Divinity of Christ in the Gospels," *Catholic Biblical Quarterly,* Vol. 24, 1962, pp. 125-139.

Clarke, Thomas E., "The Humanity of Jesus," *Commonweal,* Vol. 87, 1967, pp. 237-241.

Congar, Yves, "Real Significance of the Incarnation," *Theology Digest,* Vol. 8, 1960, pp. 74-75.

Cooper, R. M., "How Did God Become Man?" *Encounter,* Vol. 30, 1969, pp. 253-269.

Crowe, Frederick, "Christology and Contemporary Philosophy," *Commonweal,* Vol. 87, 1967, pp. 242-247.

Crowe, Frederick, "Christology, How Up to Date is Yours?" *Theological Studies,* Vol. 29, 1968, pp. 215-219.

Cullmann, Oscar, "Functional Christology: A Reply," *Theology Digest,* Vol. 10, 1962, pp. 215-219.

Dunne, John, "The Human God: Jesus," *Commonweal,* Vol. 85, 1967, pp. 508-11.

Fuch, Ernst, "Must One Believe in Jesus If He Wants to Believe in God?" *Journal for Theology and the Church,* Vol. 1, 1965, pp. 147-168.

Hamilton, William, "Good-by Chalcedon, Hello What?" *Commonweal,* Vol. 87, 1967, pp. 275-278.

Haught, John F., "What Is Logocentric Theology?" *Theological Studies,* Vol. 33, 1972, pp. 120-132.

Knox, John, *The Humanity and Divinity of Christ,* Cambridge: University Press, 1967.

Malevez, Leopold, "Functional Christology in the NT," *Theology Digest,* Vol. 10, 1962, pp. 77-83.

North, Robert, "Soul-Body Unity and God-Man Unity," *Theological Studies* Vol. 30, 1969, pp. 27-60.

North, Robert, "Recent Christology and Theological Method," *Continuum,* Vol. 7, 1969, pp. 63-77.

Rahner, Karl, "Christology Within and Evolutionary View of

the World," *Theological Investigations,* Vol. 5, Baltimore: Helicon, 1966, pp. 157-192.

————, "Current Problems in Christology," *Theological Investigations,* Vol. 1, Baltimore: Helicon, 1961, pp. 149-200.

————, "Incarnation," *Sacramentum Mundi,* New York: Herder and Herder, 1971.

————, "Jesus Christ," *Sacramentum Mundi,* New York: Herder and Herder, 1971.

————, *Spiritual Exercises,* New York: Herder and Herder, 1965.

————, "The Theology of the Incarnation," *Theological Investigations,* Vol. 4, Baltimore: Helicon, 1966, pp. 105-120.

————, "Theos in the NT," *Theological Investigations,* Vol. 1, Baltimore: Helicon, 1961, pp. 79-148.

Schoonenberg, Piet: *The Christ,* New York: Herder and Herder, 1971.

————, "God's Presence in Jesus: An Exchange of Viewpoints," *Theology Digest,* Vol. 19, 1971, pp. 29-38.

Stanley, David, "The Divinity of Christ in Hymns of the NT," *Proceedings of the SCCTSD,* Vol. 4, 1958, pp. 12-29.

Jesus, the Priest

Best, Ernest, "1 Peter 2:4-10: A Reconsideration," *Novum Testamentum,* Vol. 11, 1969, pp. 270-293.

Brown, Raymond, *Priest and Bishop,* Paramus: Paulist Press, 1970.

Bruce, F. F., "The Kerygma of Hebrews," *Interpretation,* Vol. 23, 1969, pp. 3-19.

Bruce, F. F., "Recent Contributions to the Understanding of Hebrews," *Expository Times,* Vol. 80, 1968, pp. 260-264.

Cody, A., *A History of Old Testament Priesthood,* Rome: Pontifical Biblical Institute, 1969.

Colson, Jean, *Ministre de Jesus-Christ ou le Sacerdoce D'evangile,* Paris: Beauchesne, 1966.

Crehan, Joseph, "Ministerial Priesthood," *Theological Studies,* Vol. 32, 1971, pp. 489-499.

Fransen, Piet, "The Glory of Christ," *The Way,* Vol. 5, 1965, pp. 11-22.

Higgins, A. J., "The Priestly Messiah," *New Testament Studies,* Vol. 13, 1966-7, pp. 211-239.

Leeming, Bernard, "Christ the Priest," *The Way,* Vol. 5, 1965, pp. 3-10.

Nixon, R. E., "The Biblical Idea of a Holy Nation," *Churchman,* Vol. 83, 1969, pp. 9-20.

O'Rourke, John J., "The Church as People of God in the New Testament," *Divinitas,* Vol. 13, 1969, pp. 655-668.

Schillebeeckx, E., "Catholic Understanding of Office," *Theological Studies,* Vol. 30, 1969, pp. 567-587.

Schlier, Heinrich, "New Testament Elements of Priestly Office," *Theology Digest,* Vol. 18, 1970, pp. 11-18.

Smith, J., *A Priest Forever: A Study of Typology and Eschatology in Hebrews,* London: Sheed and Ward, 1969.

Vanhoye, Albert, *Exegesis Epistulae Ad Hebraeos,* Rome: Pontifical Biblical Institute, 1968.

Von Rad, Gerhard, *Studies in Deuteronomy,* London: S.C.M. Press, 1953.

SCRIPTURAL REFERENCES

149

INDEX